Traits of Good Writing

6-8

Written by
Stella Ma, Ph.D. & June Hetzel, Ph.D.

Editor: Collene Dobelmann
Illustrator: Jenny Campbell
Designer/Production: Moonhee Pak/Carrie Rickmond
Cover Designer: Barbara Peterson
Art Director: Tom Cochrane
Project Director: Carolea Williams

© 2004 Creative Teaching Press, Inc., Huntington Beach, CA 92649
Reproduction of activities in any manner for use in the classroom and not for commercial sale is permissible.
Reproduction of these materials for an entire school or for a school system is strictly prohibited.

Table of Contents

Introduction

Each book in the *Power Practice*™ series contains dozens of ready-to-use activity pages to provide students with skill practice. Use the fun activities to supplement and enhance what you are already teaching in your classroom. Give an activity page to students as independent class work, or send the pages home as homework to reinforce skills taught in class. An answer key is included at the end of each book to provide verification of student responses.

The activity pages in *Traits of Good Writing Grades 6–8* provide an ideal way to enhance students' writing skills. The book features activities that target six important traits of writing: Ideas and Content, Organization, Voice, Word Choice, Sentence Fluency, and Conventions. These fun and challenging activities give students many opportunities to practice each writing skill in a meaningful way.

As students learn to recognize the traits of good writing, they will brainstorm and develop topics, develop and organize their thoughts and ideas, and then put their writing skills into practice. Students will gain confidence in their writing ability as they enhance grammar and usage skills and gain an awareness of how word choice and sentence development influence their wiring. As your young authors establish a style and voice of their own, they will be well on their way to becoming successful and competent writers.

Use these ready-to-go activities to "recharge" skill review and give students the power to succeed!

Writer's Notebook

BRAINSTORMING IDEAS

The topics we enjoy writing about are usually the ones that matter to us. Look for experiences and ideas that you really care about. Jot down ideas when you find them or think about them. When it comes time to write, you will have a myriad of ideas from which to choose.

Here are some prompts to get you started. Fill in each blank with an idea or recall an experience that matters to you.

Flashback: _____
Look through old photographs, letters, or souvenirs for an idea.

Favorite Place: _____
Think about a place you particularly enjoy.

It Happened to Me: _____
Think about an experience that others would be surprised by.

I Never Thought I Would: _____
Recall something you did that seemed impossible.

Remember When: _____
Reminisce about a fond memory.

If Only I Could: _____
Think about a dream you have.

Dream Vacation: _____
Where would you like your next travel adventure to take you?

Name _____ Date _____

Take Another Look
GENERATING IDEAS

Sometimes inspiration for a writing idea comes from familiar places. One place might be looking at familiar stories in a new way.

Write a short paragraph to answer questions inspired by familiar stories.

1 After Cinderella married the Prince, what apology did her stepmother give to get back in Cinderella's good graces?

_____
_____
_____
_____

2 What did Jack write in his diary after telling his mother that he sold their cow for magic beans?

_____
_____
_____
_____

3 What would Sleeping Beauty say she dreamed about during her long "nap"?

_____
_____
_____
_____

4 What would the Big Bad Wolf's mother say he was like as a Little Wolf?

_____
_____
_____
_____

Traits of Good Writing • 6–8 © 2004 Creative Teaching Press

Name _____ Date _____

Name That Genre

GENERATING IDEAS

Books are one place to find ideas for your writing. Books are organized into categories called **genres.** Science-fiction, mystery, romance, fantasy, historical fiction, and comedy are all genres. Experimenting with different genres can give you new ideas for your writing.

Label each book summary with the genre that most closely describes its type of fiction. Some genres may be used more than once.

1 Fairies, elves, and gnomes populate the world of Evergreen. Unfortunately, an evil sorcerer is threatening this peaceful land. It is up to the magical communities to save their kingdom from certain destruction. _____

2 What if you could push a button and have your next meal instantly appear? That's just what happens with the invention Mike and his father create for the science fair. Will this new device change the world or threaten to destroy it? _____

3 Can two people who meet only briefly really fall instantly in love? Sarah and Alex believe so. Follow their adventure as they spend the summer trying desperately to find each other again. _____

4 The portrait of the principal is missing and the students of Hoover Middle School want to know why. They never expected to discover that the principal disappeared as well. Can they put the pieces together in time to save their school? _____

5 Did you ever wonder what it would have been like to be Abraham Lincoln's best friend? This story imagines what the great president might have been like as a boy. Told through the eyes of a childhood friend, we see how normal the great leader may have been. _____

6 Alice just wants to go to summer camp in peace, but her siblings are determined to keep her at home. After hilarious pranks and unbelievable stunts, Alice learns just how much she is loved. _____

7 Cars that fly and buses that travel over water are a couple of the amazing ways to travel in the year 3004. You won't believe what other inventions are making life easier and more fun. _____

Traits of Good Writing • 6–8 © 2004 Creative Teaching Press

Sentence Stretch

ELABORATING ON IDEAS

> Simple sentences are the beginning of a good idea. But to really capture the reader's attention, you will need to elaborate by adding details to your sentences.

Simple sentence: The lion roared.
When: The lion roared <u>last night</u>.
Size/Color: The <u>huge, golden</u> lion roared last night.
Where: The huge, golden lion roared <u>in the jungle</u> last night.
How: The huge, golden lion roared <u>loudly</u> in the jungle last night.

"Stretch" each simple sentence by adding the following four kinds of details: when, size or color, where, and how.

1 The Ferris wheel turned around and around.

_____

2 The cat purred.

_____

3 My shoes squeaked.

_____

4 Their car stalled.

_____

5 The grocery bag ripped.

_____

6 The wind blew.

_____

7 Her school closed.

_____

Like a Person

DEVELOPING IDEAS

Personification is the technique of giving living characteristics to nonliving things. You can use personification to highlight details of an object or an abstract idea.

Consider details that describe or explain each topic. Then use those details to write a short paragraph that includes personification. Write one paragraph using your own topic idea.

Sample topic: cookie
Mrs. Cookie admitted that she was never very dependable. Her friends called her flaky. She doesn't hold up well under pressure. In fact, she has been known to crumble.

1 topic: tree

_____
_____
_____

2 topic: green

_____
_____
_____

3 topic: curiosity

_____
_____
_____

4 topic: rock

_____
_____
_____

5 topic: wind

_____
_____
_____

6 topic:

_____
_____
_____

Traits of Good Writing • 6–8 © 2004 Creative Teaching Press

Hold Up

SETTING

> The **setting** of a story may serve as the backdrop or context for an interesting plot. In this case, a story's success requires careful development of the setting. Pay attention to the words that are specific to the setting. Notice that much of the vocabulary in such a story relates to the setting.

1 Circle the nouns essential to the setting in this paragraph.

It appeared to be an ordinary day at the post office. The flag waved brightly in the breeze. Closed windows glistened in the morning sunlight. The mailbox, as always, stood proudly to the right of the main entrance, welcoming contributions. But something was wrong, Jarrod observed. The mailbag sat there on the ground unattended for at least fifteen minutes. The window blinds were never shut in the morning. Customers have entered the post office, but no one has yet left the post office. "Very strange. Very strange indeed."

Write three supporting details from the paragraph for each main idea statement.

2 **Main Idea:** It appeared to be an ordinary day at the post office.
Supporting Details:
A. _____
B. _____
C. _____

3 **Main Idea:** But something was wrong, Jarrod observed.
Supporting Details:
A. _____
B. _____
C. _____

Write your own main idea followed by three supporting details.

4 **Main Idea:** _____
Supporting Details:
A. _____
B. _____
C. _____

Crazy Characters

CHARACTERIZATION

Characters are essential to good storytelling. Oftentimes, someone you know becomes a good basis for developing an interesting character, particularly if the person has some unusual characteristics.

Use the illustration as inspiration to create a crazy character. Pay close attention to detail and write down all your ideas.

Physical Characteristics

_____
_____
_____
_____
_____

Personality Traits

_____
_____
_____
_____
_____

Habits

_____
_____
_____
_____
_____

Now think about a problem this character may have that might make a good story plot idea.

_____
_____

Name _____ Date _____

Invention Convention

One way to generate ideas is to brainstorm problem-solution scenarios. In fiction writing, you can create wild and crazy solutions that showcase your creativity!

Identify the problem and suggested solutions in the paragraph.

Many people have problems biting their fingernails. One solution would be to require them to paint their fingernails with a nasty-tasting polish. Another solution would be to require them to wear acrylic nails that are too thick to bite or tear. A final solution would be to invent the "anti-nail-biting machine." You place your fingers into a bath of soothing, vibrating warm gel ten minutes per day and close your eyes and listen to soothing music. The gel and music will be so relaxing that your nervous habit disappears. No more nail biting!

1 **Problem:** _____
Solutions:
  A. _____
  B. _____
  C. _____

Identify common problems, such as oversleeping, not completing homework, running out of money, car breaking down, or forgetting your lunch. Then, think about three possible solutions for each problem. Include a wild and crazy invention as one of your solutions to each problem.

2 **Problem:** _____
Solutions:
  A. _____
  B. _____
  C. _____

3 **Problem:** _____
Solutions:
  A. _____
  B. _____
  C. _____

4 **Problem:** _____
Solutions:
  A. _____
  B. _____
  C. _____

Traits of Good Writing • 6–8 © 2004 Creative Teaching Press

Cause and Effect

DEVELOPING CAUSE AND EFFECT

Nonfiction writing is often written in a cause-effect format. For example, a social studies passage might be about the Gold Rush and demonstrate the many effects upon California when the Gold Rush began.

The California Gold Rush of 1948 and 1949 changed the face of California. People traveled from the east coast by land or around South America by boat and crowded the port cities. Prices of food, clothing, and tools were driven up by the growing population and the presence of more currency (e.g., gold). Businesses sprang up everywhere as merchants made haste to take advantage of business opportunities. The Gold Rush was an exciting era in California where some found their fortunes and others lost everything they owned.

1 Identify cause-and-effect relationships in the paragraph.

Cause: _____
Effect: _____

Cause: _____
Effect: _____

Cause: _____
Effect: _____

Cause: _____
Effect: _____

2 Circle a problem that interests you from the list. Brainstorm possible effects of this problem.

air pollution	too much traffic	overcrowding
rise in cancer	poor eating habits	lack of exercise

Cause: _____
Effect #1: _____
Effect #2: _____
Effect #3: _____

Traits of Good Writing • 6–8 © 2004 Creative Teaching Press

Food Fair

IDEAS FROM ADVERTISEMENTS

> In the world of business, writers compose advertisements to convince potential customers to purchase products. Well-written ads include a clever product name and describe special features of the product. Convincing ads also create a sense of urgency and convince the reader that the price is affordable.

Answer the questions about the ad for June's Jumbles.

June's Jumbles

June's Jumbles will satisfy your sweet tooth while providing scrumptious, mouthwatering satisfaction. These crunchy cookies, filled with nuts, chocolate chips, and sunflower seeds, provide all-day energy—especially with a tall glass of milk. An affordable family staple with homemade quality, buy two boxes for the price of one—while supplies last!

1 Identify two cause-and-effect relationships in the ad.

Cause: _____

Effect: _____

Cause: _____

Effect: _____

2 Name four nouns and list an adjective used to describe each one.

Adjective	**Noun**
_____	_____
_____	_____
_____	_____
_____	_____

3 What statement did the author make to convince the reader that the product has an affordable price?

_____

4 What technique did the author use to create a sense of urgency?

_____

5 Based on this ad, would you purchase June's Jumbles? Why or why not?

_____

Traits of Good Writing • 6–8 © 2004 Creative Teaching Press

Break It Down

NARROWING YOUR FOCUS

Good writers move from the general to the specific. General topics and ideas can be mundane and ordinary. Narrowing your focus to a more specific idea can make your writing more interesting.

General Idea: I like to go to the beach.
Narrowed Focus: I like to surf near the Santa Monica pier on Saturday mornings.

Match each general idea with its more narrowed focus.

General Idea

_____ **1** Shopping is fun.

_____ **2** Movies are great to watch.

_____ **3** Reading is my favorite hobby.

_____ **4** I can't wait until I get my driver's license.

_____ **5** I like to ski fast.

Narrowed Focus

A. Reading the book *A Tree Grows in Brooklyn* reminded me why reading is one of my favorite hobbies.

B. Spending my entire allowance at Fashion Island shopping center is my favorite weekend activity.

C. Nothing compares to skiing down a snowy slope and pretending you are the gold-metal favorite in a slalom race.

D. When I get my driver's license, the first thing I will do is drive around my neighborhood honking like I'm in a parade.

E. I like to munch on a huge bucket of popcorn while watching *The Terminator.*

Narrow each general idea.

6 Dolphins swim in the ocean.

_____

7 Rainy days are boring.

_____

8 My friends are nice.

_____

9 Dogs are usually friendly.

_____

Name _____ Date _____

Biography Blizzard
IMPORTANT DETAILS

> **Biographies** capture who, what, when, where, and why of a person's life. When writing a biography, it is important to choose pivotal events that will describe the person's character. Chronological order helps the biography read like a story.

Read the timeline. Select important details and events to include in a short biography of Wilma Rudolph. Organize the events in the paragraph in chronological order.

 Wilma Rudolph is born in Clarksville, TN.
- She was the 20th of 22 children.
- Wilma's mother was a maid.
- Her father worked for the railroad.

 Wilma is diagnosed with polio.
- Wilma experiences many other childhood illnesses, leaving her left leg paralyzed.
- Wilma's mother took her for weekly therapy.
- She rubbed Wilma's leg and taught her other children to do the same.

 Wilma is able to walk with a leg brace.

 Wilma plays basketball for her school.
- A track coach convinced her to run track in her senior year in high school.

 Wilma was selected for the U.S. Olympic track team and ran in Melbourne, Australia.
- She won a bronze medal.

1960 **Wilma ran in the Olympics in Rome and won three gold medals.**

 Wilma retires from running.
- Wilma started the Wilma Rudolph Foundation to help children learn about discipline and hard work.

1994 **Wilma Rudolph died of brain cancer.**

_____
_____
_____
_____
_____
_____
_____
_____
_____
_____
_____
_____
_____
_____
_____
_____
_____
_____
_____
_____
_____
_____
_____
_____
_____
_____
_____
_____
_____
_____
_____
_____
_____

Traits of Good Writing • 6–8 © 2004 Creative Teaching Press

Name _____ Date _____

Topic Turmoil

> The **topic sentence** states the main idea of the paragraph. It sets the mood for the paragraph and lets the reader know what information will follow.

Read each pair of words and write a topic sentence for a paragraph that would compare and contrast those items.

1 whales—dolphins

_____

2 football—basketball

_____

3 North America—South America

_____

4 earth—moon

_____

5 cats—dogs

_____

6 ants—spiders

_____

For each idea write a topic sentence that states your opinion and could be used to begin a persuasive paragraph.

7 banning soda in school

_____

8 lengthening the school day

_____

9 mandatory school uniforms

_____

10 restricting students' access to violent video games

_____

Experiencing Details

KINDS OF DETAILS

> When gathering details, you often use your personal experiences. You may use your senses, your memory, or your imagination.
> **Sensory** details come from your own senses (smell, touch, taste, hearing, and sight).
> **Memory** details come from past experiences or observations.
> **Reflective** details come from the creative thought or imagination of the writer.

Identify each kind of detail. Write **S** if it is a sensory detail, **M** if it is a memory detail, or **R** if it is a reflective detail.

_____ **1** In the summer, we slept outside when we visited my grandmother.

_____ **2** I wonder what the surface of the moon is like.

_____ **3** Last year, the eighth graders went on a trip to the state capital.

_____ **4** The watermelon tasted sweet and juicy.

_____ **5** Our coach sounds as tough as he looks.

_____ **6** I hope we have good seats in the auditorium.

_____ **7** I wish we could go on a long family vacation.

_____ **8** When I was little, I loved to catch fireflies.

_____ **9** The cold floor made my toes feel like ice cubes.

_____ **10** The noise was so loud that my teeth were vibrating.

_____ **11** Yesterday, Mr. Swanson gave everyone an extra assignment.

_____ **12** I wonder how many times I can swim across the lake.

_____ **13** I could smell my mother's perfume as soon as we entered the house.

_____ **14** I remember the way we folded the paper to make the beautiful swan.

_____ **15** Someday I hope to write a novel.

_____ **16** Last week, I saw a caterpillar make a cocoon.

_____ **17** The car engine sounded like a roaring lion.

_____ **18** The lemons tasted bitter on my tongue.

_____ **19** I wish we could climb all the trees in the nature park.

_____ **20** I wonder how many blocks it would take to build a tower to the ceiling.

Traits of Good Writing • 6–8 © 2004 Creative Teaching Press

Name _____ Date _____

Give Texture to Your Writing

IDENTIFYING SUPPORTING DETAILS

When you write a paragraph, start with a topic sentence that includes the main idea. Then, provide supporting sentences to bring "texture" and depth to your writing.

Draw an X beside each sentence that provides a detail that supports the main idea (topic sentence).

Topic sentence: Rosebushes can be one of the most rewarding flowers to grow.

_____ **1** The green foliage provides a lovely backdrop for the bright red blossoms.

_____ **2** Stargazer lilies have a beautiful fragrance.

_____ **3** Tulips paired with daisies make a stunning bouquet.

_____ **4** The velvety texture of the brilliant red petals and the delicately perfumed scent make lovely potpourri.

_____ **5** Soil comes in many varieties.

_____ **6** Pruning your rosebushes once a year helps shape the plants.

_____ **7** Cultivating roses may become your favorite hobby, provided you wear gardening gloves to protect your fingers from sharp thorns.

Topic sentence: Playing professional roller hockey has been Lori's lifelong dream.

_____ **1** Roller rinks are usually closed on Sunday nights.

_____ **2** For practice, Lori skates three or four days a week on a beachside path.

_____ **3** Her hockey fever is infectious.

_____ **4** Holding her first trophy, Lori glides across the concrete rink on her inline skates.

_____ **5** When Lori first began, she signed up for a hockey class.

_____ **6** There was controversy over a scored goal.

_____ **7** Lori competed in her first tournament in 1994.

Which One Doesn't Belong?

SORTING DETAILS

Read each topic sentence. Then, read the list of details. Identify which detail does NOT support the main idea. Draw an X in the blank before the unnecessary detail.

1 **Topic sentence:** Color affects mood and behavior.
_____ Children in red classrooms are more aggressive
_____ Blue makes people feel calm.
_____ Red and yellow are primary colors.
_____ A yellow kitchen stimulates appetite.

2 **Topic sentence:** Organized athletic programs benefit students.
_____ Student athletes perform well on standardized tests.
_____ Athletes learn about health and wellness.
_____ Sporting equipment is expensive.
_____ Many student athletes go on to college.

3 **Topic sentence:** E-mail is the best way to keep in touch.
_____ Handwritten notes are more personal.
_____ E-mail is immediate.
_____ Near real-time conversation can take place with e-mail.
_____ Photographs can be included in an e-mail.

4 **Topic sentence:** Traveling by car is the most popular method of transportation.
_____ More families drive than fly for vacations.
_____ Gas prices may vary by region.
_____ Cars provide an affordable and accessible means of transportation.
_____ It is easy to go most places by car.

5 **Topic sentence:** Learning to play piano is one of the biggest achievements of my life.
_____ I learned to ride my bicycle when I was in first grade.
_____ I have had hours of enjoyment from playing piano.
_____ I earned a scholarship in music from a four-year college.
_____ Practicing piano each day taught me discipline.

6 **Topic sentence:** Mike and Andrea were excited about their new puppy.
_____ Andrea bought a collar and water dish with her own money.
_____ Mike rushed home from school each day to walk the puppy.
_____ They told all their friends about their new pet.
_____ Mike is allergic to cats.

Name _____ Date _____

Unpack Your Ideas

TOPIC SENTENCE/SUPPORTING DETAILS

When you write a descriptive paragraph "unpack your ideas" by including a topic sentence along with supporting details. Use descriptive clauses, metaphors, or similes to give the details interest.

Topic Sentence: From the southern lookout, the panorama of Yosemite Valley met our eyes.

Supporting Details:
This glacial valley boasts of magnificent, granite mountains and cascading waterfalls on both sides. To the right we see Bridal Veil Falls with Half Dome, a giant sentinel in the background. To the left El Capitan dominates the skyline, towering next to the thunderous Yosemite Falls. There is no other place on earth with such a breathtaking view as the southern perspective of Yosemite Valley.

Identify the proper nouns that form the foundation of the main idea in this paragraph.

Complete the descriptive phrases that support the main idea.

1 _____
2 _____
3 _____
4 _____
5 _____

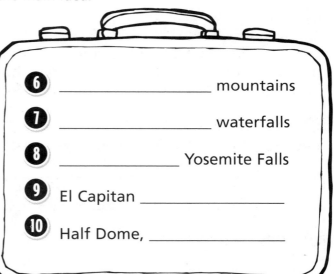

6 _____ mountains
7 _____ waterfalls
8 _____ Yosemite Falls
9 El Capitan _____
10 Half Dome, _____

Select a place you have recently visited or would like to visit, and write a descriptive paragraph about it. Remember to begin with a topic sentence.

11 **Topic Sentence:** _____

Supporting Details:
_____
_____
_____
_____

Traits of Good Writing • 6–8 © 2004 Creative Teaching Press

Picture Perfect!

DEVELOPING PARAGRAPHS

When you write a paragraph, make it picture perfect by including a topic sentence with the main idea and supporting sentences that describe the details.

Details:
- Oregon coast
- craggy cliffs
- crashing waves
- moonlight
- foghorn sounding
- turning light
- reflection of light off the surface of the waves
- ship in distance

Paragraph:
The lighthouse stood on the craggy cliff overlooking the Oregon coast. Waves crashed as the moonlight reflected off the water. The foghorn moaned to the beat of the turning signal light. In the distance, a lone ship found its way safely around the cape.

Use the following topic and details to write a descriptive paragraph of your own.

Details:
- steel
- thrilling speed
- sharp curves
- breathtaking dives
- sounds of screams
- rushing wind in your face

Paragraph:

_____

_____

_____

_____

Traits of Good Writing • 6–8 © 2004 Creative Teaching Press

In a Nutshell

Summary Statements

Summary statements can be challenging to write. Summaries capture the main idea without getting bogged down in too many details.

Notes:
Whales live in the ocean.
There are two categories of whales.
Orcas, grays, minkes, and humpbacks are types of whales.
Toothed whales, one main group, eat meat.
Baleen whales, another main group, are filter feeders.

Summary statement: Whales come in a variety of shapes and sizes and are divided into two main groups, toothed and baleen.

Write summary statements for the next two sets of facts.

Notes:
John Muir was born in Scotland in 1838.
Muir moved to a farm when he was eleven.
John Muir was a naturalist and a photographer.
John Muir loved Yosemite.
He co-founded the Sierra Club in 1892.
Muir established thirteen forest reserves.
Muir spent much of his life protecting natural areas.

Summary statement: _____
_____
_____
_____

Notes:
California is on the west coast of the United States.
San Francisco, San Diego, and Long Beach are large port cities.
Hollywood boasts the movie-making industry.
Central California, composed of farms, is the food basket of the state.
Northern and Central California have many wineries.
Sacramento is the state capital.

Summary statement: _____
_____
_____
_____

Traits of Good Writing • 6–8 © 2004 Creative Teaching Press

Name _____ Date _____

Writer's Lingo

WRITER'S TERMINOLOGY

Use the words in the word box to complete the crossword puzzle.

summary	chronological	causes	lead	conclusion
outline	author	idea	plot	problem

Across
2. When you write a story in sequence, it means you are writing the story in _____ order.
4. The beginning, or _____, of a story should catch the reader's attention.
5. The concluding or _____ paragraph comes at the end of an essay.
7. The story _____ includes the beginning, rising action, climax, falling action, and resolution.
9. Before you write a report or an essay, it is helpful to brainstorm your ideas and _____ your points.

Down
1. One organizational writing structure is called _____-solution.
2. The ending of a story is called the _____.
3. The effects in a story are a result of the _____.
6. The person who writes the story is called the _____.
8. To make a story good, you need to start with a good _____.

Traits of Good Writing • 6–8 © 2004 Creative Teaching Press

Grab the Reader's Interest

STRONG STORY BEGINNINGS

> Strong story beginnings grab the reader's attention and interest, arousing curiosity. An effective opening paragraph immediately propels the reader into the plot.

Read the leads and write your own lead for a story using a similar technique.

1 "Where's Papa going with that ax?" said Fern to her mother as they were setting the table for breakfast.
"Out to the hoghouse," replied Mrs. Arable. "Some pigs were born last night."
—*Charlotte's Web* by E.B. White

Did the lead from *Charlotte's Web* arouse your curiosity?   Yes No
Write your own story beginning using dialogue. Arouse the curiosity of the reader.

_____

_____

_____

2 "Maniac Magee was not born in a dump. He was born in a house, a pretty ordinary house, right across the river from here, in Bridgeport. And he had regular parents, a mother and a father. But not for long."
—*Maniac Magee* by Jerry Spinelli

Did the lead from *Maniac Magee* arouse your curiosity?   Yes   No
Write your own story beginning using suspense to grab the reader's attention.

_____

_____

_____

Discover some other interesting story beginnings. Pick two of your favorite books. Copy the beginning sentences below.

Book Title: _____

Beginning: _____

_____

Book Title: _____

Beginning: _____

_____

Name _____ Date _____

In the News

Strong Story Beginnings

Newspaper articles should begin with a strong lead or opening statement. The lead summarizes the main points of the news story in one or two sentences. News writers often develop the lead by asking themselves the questions *who, what, why, where, when,* and *how.* They then put the answers to these questions—or at least the important questions—into the opening of the story.

Read each news article lead. Write **S** on the line if you think the lead is strong. Write **W** if you think the lead is weak.

_____ **1** Student body president Mindy Oaks told classmates Thursday that the senior fund was broke and the class trip was in jeopardy of being canceled.

_____ **2** In this article you will find out how the car in the accident drove over the curb and into the house.

_____ **3** Someone found the fish dead when they arrived at school. The fish belonged to Mr. Sennet. He is the fifth grade teacher. The power went out last night, so that might have been the problem.

_____ **4** A girl's mountain bike, a helmet, and a tire pump were stolen early Monday morning from the garage of Helen Rodgers, according to Police Chief Albert Miller. The equipment was valued at more than three hundred dollars.

_____ **5** Coach Carter said the girls played hard. It is too bad that they didn't win. The soccer team only scored one goal yesterday. The team only lost one other game this year. The other team scored four goals. That makes them the girl's soccer team with the most wins in one year.

Look at the leads you identified as strong. Why do you think they were effective in arousing the interest of the reader?

_____

_____

_____

Choose one lead that you felt was NOT effective. Rewrite it to make it effective.

_____

_____

_____

Traits of Good Writing • 6–8 © 2004 Creative Teaching Press

Get the Point!

THESIS STATEMENTS

The **thesis** of an essay states the main points. It helps the reader know what to expect in the passage. The thesis statement presents the main purpose of the writing and sets up the organization of what is to come.

Underline the thesis statement in each paragraph. List the main points from the thesis.

1 Many students struggle to keep up with their homework. Some become too involved with other activities, such as spending time with friends, talking on the phone, watching television, or playing video games. Learning how to set priorities, avoid distractions, and create a reward system will help students improve their homework management skills.

What are the three main points of the thesis statement?
A. _____
B. _____
C. _____

2 Kindness is an important and valuable character trait. It makes a person attractive and people generally want to be friends with those who treat them well. You can demonstrate kindness by asking people how they are doing, listening to what they tell you, and thinking of creative ways to help others.

What are the three main points of the thesis statement?
A. _____
B. _____
C. _____

3 Recycling is good for the Earth. Every community needs to have a quality recycling program in place. Creating a recycling program requires carefully analyzing the community's needs, sharing information with all community members, and providing support for people as they begin to recycle in their homes and businesses.

What are the three main points of the thesis statement?
A. _____
B. _____
C. _____

Traits of Good Writing • 6–8 © 2004 Creative Teaching Press

Name _____   Date _____

Wide Angle and Close-Up

ORGANIZING INFORMATION

> Try organizing your writing ideas by focusing on the wide angle shot (big, first-impression details) and then moving to the close-ups (smaller, more intricate details).

Read the details about the room. Categorize each detail as wide angle or close-up. Write each sentence in the correct category.

A. The bright, lively room was painted a brilliant yellow.
B. The yellow eraser on the tip of my pencil reminded me of a sunflower.
C. I could see the dust that had collected between the floor tiles.
D. I noticed the smell of baking bread all around the room.
E. The furniture was arranged on the edges of the room, leaving a large space in the middle.
F. The sunlight sent a warm glow over all the people in the room.
G. A piece of writing paper peeked out of one closed desk.
H. A spider had built a web in the corner near the window.

Wide Angle

_____

_____

_____

_____

Close-Up

_____

_____

_____

_____

Traits of Good Writing • 6–8 © 2004 Creative Teaching Press

Magnetic Writing

SEQUENCING INFORMATION

How-to writing includes step-by-step procedures. Specific direction words, such as *up, down, left, right,* and number words are important for clarity. Transitional words, such as *first, next,* and *then,* are important to establish sequence. How-to writing is direct with simple word choice.

Read the journal entry written by a scientist. Translate the list of steps from her science experiment into a paragraph that can be included in a science textbook. You will need to use direction and transitional words to make the paragraph clear.

How to Make Paper Clips Dance

Supplies:
4-inch steel bolt
Nut to fit bolt
6.5 feet of bell wire
two #6 dry cell batteries
20 paper clips

Directions:
1. Put nut on bolt end.

2. Beginning 12 inches in on the wire, wrap wire tightly around bolt from the head down.

3. Wrap until you reach the nut.

4. Continue wrapping up and down to achieve three to four layers of wire.

5. Attach an end of wire to one of the posts on top of dry cell battery.

6. Pile paper clips on table.

7. Have assistant touch other end of wire to second terminal while you hold bolt end over paper clips.

8. Watch paper clips "dance."

_____
_____
_____
_____
_____
_____
_____
_____

Name _____ Date _____

Hobby City

CHRONOLOGICAL ORDER

> Paragraphs that describe how someone does something must be written in chronological order so that the reader can track the writer's ideas.

Number each set of sentences so that each set could become a logically ordered paragraph.

The Writer

_____ At the conference she learned tips about how to get organized, how to write query letters, and how to write book proposals.

_____ Beverly always wanted to be a writer.

_____ Within a few years, she was a published writer!

_____ First, she kept a journal to practice recording her thoughts, ideas, and observations.

_____ Second, she went to a writer's conference.

_____ Then, she began to practice her new skills.

The Gardener

_____ She repeated the steps for all seven terra cotta pots and then beautifully arranged the pots in her garden patio.

_____ After this, she dug a hole in the center of the soil and gently placed one of the flowers in the hole.

_____ Deborah drove to Garden Center and purchased soil, flowers, and terra cotta pots.

_____ She then drove home and put on her gloves and work clothes.

_____ Then, she filled the pot almost full with soil.

_____ She carefully filled the rest of the hole with soil and then gingerly watered the flower.

_____ She carefully lay gravel at the bottom of each pot for proper water drainage.

The Remote Control Pilot

_____ "Building this plane was a lot of fun!"

_____ Geoff drove to Hobby Shack.

_____ Once he finished the wings, he glued the wings to the fuselage.

_____ Once there, he purchased glue, bolsa wood, Styrofoam, and plastic sheets.

_____ He drove home to build his remote control airplane.

_____ After building the fuselage out of bolsa wood, he began to work on the wings.

_____ For one of the finishing touches, Geoff used a tiny iron to melt the plastic over the bolsa wood, creating a very light, effective aircraft.

_____ "I'm almost finished," Geoff called out.

Traits of Good Writing • 6–8 © 2004 Creative Teaching Press

Name _____ Date _____

Life Events

Use the events to write a chronological paragraph about Thomas Alva Edison. You will need to create a topic sentence and a concluding sentence. Don't forget to use transitional words.

 Event One: Thomas Alva Edison was born in Milan, Ohio.

 Event Two: He worked as a telegraph operator.

 Event Three: He patented his first invention, the Electrical Vote Recorder, and then moved to New York City to start a telegraph manufacturing business.

 Event Four: Edison invented the carbon button transmitter for use in the telephone and invented the phonograph.

 Event Five: He founded the Edison Electric Light Company and began mass-producing light bulbs.

 Event Six: Edison continued to create revolutionary inventions like wireless telegraphy, the first motion picture camera, and the nickel-iron-alkaline battery until his death in 1931 at the age of 84.

Topic Sentence: _____

_____
_____
_____
_____
_____
_____
_____
_____
_____
_____
_____

Concluding Sentence: _____

Traits of Good Writing • 6–8 © 2004 Creative Teaching Press

Calculated Conclusions

PROBLEM-SOLUTION

> Much of nonfiction writing is organized in a problem-solution format. The writer first describes the problem and then one or more solutions. Fiction writing can also be organized in a problem-solution format. In fiction, the writer usually uses the characters and a variety of circumstances to bring about a solution.

Read about each problem and then complete the paragraph by writing a solution that demonstrates a calculated conclusion on the part of each character.

Mount St. Helens: Not Again!
Leena had lived on a wheat farm during the Mount St. Helens volcanic eruption in Washington. She remembered how scared she was and how people were killed or lost their property. Now that she is an adult and married, her husband wants to purchase a farm near another potentially active volcano. Leena will . . .

_____
_____
_____
_____
_____
_____
_____
_____
_____

Enrique and Henry: Friends or Foes?
Enrique is one of the smartest students in his class. He always gets A's on his papers and the other students look up to him. Now there is a new student in class named Henry. Henry has moved in from another neighborhood. Henry makes fun of Enrique being smart and, because he has such a clever sense of humor, some of the other kids are starting to like Henry and go along with his antics. The humor is cruel and Enrique is feeling hurt; however, Enrique is a very strong, self-confident person. Enrique will . . .

_____
_____
_____
_____
_____
_____
_____
_____

Traits of Good Writing • 6–8 © 2004 Creative Teaching Press

Name _____ Date _____

Weighty Arguments
Persuasive Essays

The author of a persuasive essay tries to convince an audience of his or her opinion regarding a certain topic. When you write a persuasive essay, choose at least three reasons to convince your readers of your opinion.

Thesis: Exercise is important and good for you.

1 Place an X beside the three strongest arguments that support the thesis.
___ Exercise strengthens your muscles and bones.
___ Exercise is a lot of work.
___ Exercise alone will lead to weight loss.
___ Exercise improves your blood circulation.
___ Exercise is a great way to relieve stress.
___ Exercise makes you sweat and increases water loss.

2 Order the arguments that support the thesis. Place the strongest reason at the end, the weakest in the middle, and the second strongest reason at the beginning.
___ Exercise is necessary for maintaining a healthy heart.
___ Exercise is needed to build your muscles and bones.
___ Exercise is a great way to relieve stress.

Write three supporting arguments for each thesis statement. Place your strongest argument last.

3 **Thesis: It is important to get high grades in school.**
A. _____
B. _____
C. _____

4 **Thesis: Rain forests are valuable resources and should be treasured.**
A. _____
B. _____
C. _____

Traits of Good Writing • 6–8 © 2004 Creative Teaching Press

Vote for Me

PERSUASIVE SPEECHES

Campaign speeches are a form of persuasive writing. The author tries to convince an audience of his or her opinion regarding a certain issue or topic. When you write a persuasive speech, choose at least three main arguments to convince your reader or listener of your position.

1 Create a campaign poster for each of the phrases you think are persuasive in convincing students to vote for you for class president. Draw a line through the least convincing arguments.

- involved with many student activities
- most popular girls in class are my friends
- ran a successful fund-raising project for the class
- will listen to your concerns
- maintaining good grades
- our principal likes me the best of all the candidates

2 Order the arguments according to their importance. Place the strongest argument third, the weakest second, and the second strongest argument first.
___ I will listen to your concerns.
___ I'm involved with many school activities.
___ I am generally a good student and maintain good grades.

3 Combine all three of your arguments into one campaign statement.
Vote for me for class president because . . .

_____

_____

Traits of Good Writing • 6–8 © 2004 Creative Teaching Press

Name _____ Date _____

Category Sort

Organizing Information

Organizing nonfiction information by content areas will make your writing clear and logical. Create subcategories for your facts and then develop each subcategory into a well-crafted paragraph.

Sort the facts about black bears into three categories.
    A. Diet   **B.** Habitat   **C.** Appearance

1 _____ They den for winter sleep in the northern parts of their range.

2 _____ There is a distinct white patch on the chest, which is sometimes in the shape of a V.

3 _____ Black bears feed on a wide range of foods, including fruit, bees' nests, insects, invertebrates, and small vertebrates.

4 _____ In summer, they have been reported at altitudes over 9,900 feet (3,000 m).

5 _____ The degree to which they prey on wild, hoofed mammals is unknown.

6 _____ This medium-sized, black-colored bear has a light-colored muzzle and ears which appear large in proportion to the rest of its head.

7 _____ The black bear has a patch of white on the chin.

8 _____ In fall, they frequently make crude, leafy feeding platforms in nut-bearing trees.

9 _____ Black bears live predominantly in forested areas, especially in hills and mountainous areas.

Use the sorted facts to write three well-crafted paragraphs about black bears. Use the back of this page if you need more writing space.

_____
_____
_____
_____
_____
_____
_____

Traits of Good Writing • 6–8 © 2004 Creative Teaching Press

Name _____ Date _____

Managing Internet Searches
ORGANIZING RESEARCH

> The Internet provides a wealth of resources for planning and organizing your writing. One common use of the Internet is finding research to support the topic of your writing. The easiest way to find information is to conduct a keyword search. When you use a keyword to search, you will then need to sort through all the resulting information to find those articles that are most useful to your purpose.

Read each topic. Circle the keyword(s) that would NOT be useful in your search.

1 history of dogs
     A. dog history   **B.** dog supplies   **C.** pets in America

2 Amelia Earhart
     A. women in aviation   **B.** famous women   **C.** mysteries

3 current baseball players
     A. history of baseball   **B.** Major League Baseball   **C.** baseball news

4 mosquitoes
     A. insect pests   **B.** winter bugs   **C.** outdoor pest control

After running a search for *Mexico,* the search engine provided the following Web sites. Write the letter of the site or sites that best answers each question.

A. Travel City: Mexican Vacations: the ultimate resource to plan and enjoy your vacation
B. Flavors of Mexico: complete listing of authentic Mexican recipes, including historical background
C. A Cultural History of Mexico: a look at the art and artists of Mexico, including music, dance, and visual arts
D. MexOnline: The Complete Online Guide to Mexico: the most complete online guide to Mexico, including accommodations, activities, business, culture, history, real estate
E. CIA—The World Factbook—Mexico: synopsis of most recent field research on geography, people, economy, transportation, military

_____ **5** Which site or sites would you use to plan a trip to Mexico?

_____ **6** Which site would provide the most up-to-date information about Mexico?

_____ **7** Which site would give you a recipe for tostadas?

_____ **8** Where would you look to find information on the history of mariachi bands?

_____ **9** Where could you find the names of current government officials?

_____ **10** Which site or sites would give you the major industries in Mexico?

Traits of Good Writing • 6–8 © 2004 Creative Teaching Press

Name _____ Date _____

Get Your Facts Straight

ORGANIZING RESEARCH

Once you have found research to support your main idea, you will need to organize that information into a plan for writing.

Read each of the following facts about Mexico. Organize each fact by writing its letter in the appropriate category in the outline.

Facts about Mexico

A. President is chief executive officer
B. borders the Caribbean Sea and the Gulf of Mexico
C. tortilla is a Mexican flat bread
D. mountains, plateaus, low coastal plains, and deserts
E. Constitution adopted on February 5, 1917
F. mariachi is a type of traditional Mexican music
G. Cinco de Mayo commemorates victory over the French Army
H. Federal republic
I. traditional Mexican foods include guacamole, enchiladas, tostadas, quesadillas
J. Mexico is known for its meat dishes
K. the "huapango" is a dance from Veracruz
L. climate varies from tropical to desert
M. legislative branch is bicameral National Congress
N. gained independence from Spain on September 16, 1810

I. Geography

_____

_____

_____

II. History

_____

_____

_____

III. Government

_____

_____

_____

IV. Cultural Arts

_____

_____

V. Food

_____

_____

_____

Traits of Good Writing • 6–8 © 2004 Creative Teaching Press

Transition Chart

TRANSITIONAL WORDS

Transitions are words or phrases that connect details and ideas in writing. Transitional words can be organized into different categories. Choosing the correct transitional words for your writing will strengthen your organization.

Write each word or phrase in the word box under the correct category in the chart.

similarly	amid	finally	in the meantime
in back of	otherwise	beneath	in conclusion
first	even so	as a result	in the same way
to sum up	after a while	however	above

Transitions that show location

_____
_____
_____
_____
_____
_____
_____
_____

Transitions that compare and contrast

_____
_____
_____
_____
_____
_____
_____
_____

Transitions that show time

_____
_____
_____
_____
_____
_____

Transitions that conclude or summarize

_____
_____
_____
_____
_____
_____

Traits of Good Writing • 6–8 © 2004 Creative Teaching Press

Find That Transition

TRANSITIONAL WORDS

Read the passage. Underline the transitional words and phrases.

   Camping is one of the best ways to vacation, but preparation is everything. Before you leave, you must plan and pack well. I always lay out all my clothes and supplies so I can double-check everything.

   Next, I remember to bring only necessary items. This is especially important if you must hike to your campsite. Even so, adding an extra sweater or blanket is never a bad idea. Some nights can get chilly.

   When you arrive at your site, be sure to scope out the facilities—first the restrooms and water supply. Try to pitch your tent near these important areas. You don't want long hikes in the middle of the night. On the other hand, you don't want to be too close to these areas. Otherwise, you will constantly be disturbed by other campers.

Once you have set up camp, go out and enjoy yourself. Take some relaxing walks, or just sit and listen to the music of nature. However, always remember to respect the land. Never leave any trash behind. That way, your magical vacation spot will remain so for many visits to come.

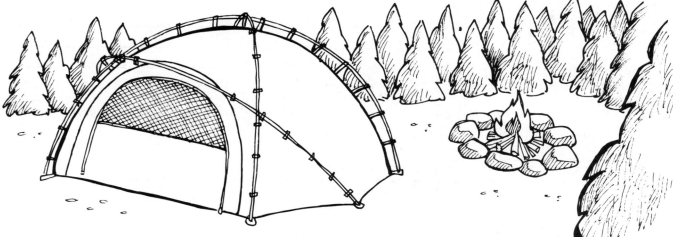

Choose four transitional words from the text above. Use each in a sentence below.

1 _____

2 _____

3 _____

4 _____

Traits of Good Writing • 6–8 © 2004 Creative Teaching Press

In Other Words

Writing Conclusions

Conclusions end an essay and restate the thesis. When a conclusion restates the thesis (main points of the essay), the author uses different words so that the introduction and conclusion review content but are not redundant.

Thesis Statement
It's important to cultivate friendships because everyone needs a peer group, friends with whom you can share common interests, and people who will be there for you during difficult times.

Restatement of Thesis within Concluding Paragraph
Friendship creates a wonderful support because you have people with whom you can spend time, people who enjoy the same things that you enjoy, and friends who will support you during rough times.

Restate each thesis statement.

1 Basketball is my favorite sport because it is fast moving, requires a great deal of skill, and involves team play.

_____
_____
_____

2 When you buy your first car you should consider the price, comfort and style, and reliability.

_____
_____
_____

3 Do not trust people with severe character flaws, such as those who lie, steal, or cheat.

_____
_____
_____

4 A skin care system is important for several reasons, including keeping clean, maintaining a youthful look, and preventing too much sun exposure.

_____
_____
_____

Traits of Good Writing • 6–8 © 2004 Creative Teaching Press

It's a Wrap

WRITING CONCLUSIONS

An ending rounds out writing, ties up details, and leaves the reader with a feeling of satisfaction and resolution. There are many techniques you can use to end your writing, including
- a laugh
- a challenge to take action
- a literary device, such as a metaphor
- a surprise
- a quote or profound thought

Read each topic sentence. Use one of the techniques listed above to write a satisfactory ending statement. Be creative and try using a different technique for each idea.

1 If you want to know how not to train your new puppy, then spend an hour with my sister and her dog Meatball.

_____
_____
_____

2 Learning to play a musical instrument is a rewarding life experience.

_____
_____
_____

3 I'll never forget the day I met the President of the United States.

_____
_____
_____

4 The Rocky Mountains are a beautiful sight to behold and filled with amazing adventures.

_____
_____
_____

5 I never imagined how important my first-aid skills would be until I finally needed them.

_____
_____
_____

Name _____ Date _____

Rocket Writing

FIVE-PARAGRAPH ESSAYS

Five-paragraph essays can easily be organized around a rocket! Use the rocket writing graphic organizer to visually remember how to write an introductory paragraph, three supporting middle paragraphs, and a concluding paragraph. Label each part of the essay using words from the word box.

| restatement of thesis | conclusion | introduction | point two |
| point three | thesis statement | point one | |

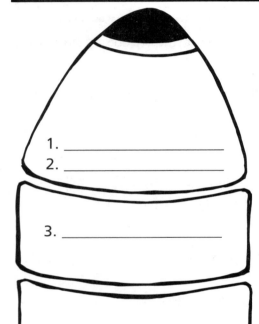

1. _____
2. _____

3. _____

4. _____

5. _____

6. _____
7. _____

What would life be like without a best friend? Everybody needs a best friend with whom they can hang out, have fun, and discuss all their concerns.

Best friends spend time together. Sometimes I go to my best friend's house. Sometimes he comes to my apartment. On the weekends, we like to go to the park.

Best friends also have a lot of fun together. Sometimes my best friend and I play basketball. Other times we play soccer. Sometimes we just play video games or watch television.

Best friends can also discuss concerns. When my dad died, I could tell my best friend how sad I was. He listened and I really appreciated it. At first it was hard to say how I felt, but my best friend understood. He doesn't have a dad either.

Life is better when you share it with a friend. Let your best friend know how much you enjoy spending time together, how much fun you have when you are together, and how thankful you are that you can share all your cares.

Traits of Good Writing • 6–8 © 2004 Creative Teaching Press

Name _____ Date _____

Bon Appétit!

DIRECT SPEECH

> **Direct speech** is the repeating of speech by giving exact words that were spoken. Quotation marks are usually used.
> **Indirect speech** is a report of something said or written but not the exact words in original form. It is also called *indirect discourse* or *reported speech.*

Check the sentence(s) that represent direct speech statements.

_____ **1** You must try the China Palace downtown if you like gourmet Chinese food.

_____ **2** The food critic wrote, "I found the seafood dishes outstanding in taste and presentation."

_____ **3** The show host asked her guest if she preferred Chinese or Italian food.

_____ **4** Their neighbor recommended China Palace for fine dining in the traditional Oriental style.

Rewrite the sentences into direct quotes. Don't forget to add the appropriate quotation and end marks.

5 I informed the viewers that China Palace was recently given a five-star rating by five of the top food magazines.

_____

_____

6 I announced that Mrs. Chan would be showing the viewers how to prepare one of her specialties, walnut shrimp, which also happens to be the host's favorite menu item.

_____

_____

7 My guest, Mrs. Chan, asked me why I preferred the walnut shrimp dish to the other items on her restaurant's menu.

_____

_____

8 My answer to Mrs. Chan's question about why I liked her walnut shrimp the best was that her special sauce made the dish taste unique; tangy, creamy and honey sweet.

_____

_____

Traits of Good Writing • 6–8 © 2004 Creative Teaching Press

Wok Express

INDIRECT SPEECH

> **Indirect speech** is a report of something said or written but not the exact words in original form. It is also called *indirect discourse* or *reported speech.*

Check the sentence(s) that represent indirect speech.

_____ **1** You are late! The black bean chicken and rice was ready an hour ago.

_____ **2** He told me that he saw Jim buying a large burger with fries.

_____ **3** Jim said that he preferred a home-cooked meal to fast food.

_____ **4** I ate the burger because I was hungry.

Welcome to a famous cooking show! Imagine that you are recounting what you saw on the show to your neighbor who missed the show. Rewrite the following dialog using indirect speech or reported speech.

5 "Good evening everyone. I am your host, Nora Cooke."

_____

_____

6 "Viewers, welcome to *Wok Express*, the top Chinese cooking show on public television."

_____

_____

7 "Let's meet Mrs. Chan, our guest cook today."

_____

_____

8 "Mrs. Chan has been a restaurant chef for many years at the China Place."

_____

_____

Traits of Good Writing • 6–8 © 2004 Creative Teaching Press

Dear Madam

FIRST PERSON

Writing in the first person uses the first person pronoun, *I*. This may be used in direct speech or autobiographical writing.

Practice developing your voice. Write a letter to your principal on behalf of your class, requesting that lessons be cancelled tomorrow so that your class can support your basketball team. The game is the final game of the season and half of the team players are in your class.

Dear Ms. McKane,

_____
_____
_____
_____
_____
_____
_____
_____

Yours sincerely,

_____

You are now the principal of the school. Respond to the student's letter above by writing a letter refusing the request. Provide two reasons for your decision.

Dear _____,

_____
_____
_____
_____
_____
_____
_____

Yours sincerely,

_____

Traits of Good Writing • 6–8 © 2004 Creative Teaching Press

Name _____ Date _____

Out of Town

FIRST/SECOND/THIRD PERSON

> Writing in the first person uses the first person pronoun, *I*. Writing in the second person uses the second person pronoun, *you*. Writing in the third person usually uses third person pronouns, such as *they, it, he,* or *she.*

Circle the correct voice for each sentence.

1 You must come over for a meal when you finish.
first   second   third

2 He left last night to visit his cousins in Kentucky.
first   second   third

3 You agreed to look after the garden and the dogs in their absence.
first   second   third

4 They were given the responsibility of feeding the birds.
first   second   third

5 Sorry, I'm not available for babysitting this week.
first   second   third

Convert these first person statements into second person statements.

6 I turned off the water sprinklers after the rain.

_____

_____

7 Then I checked the dogs to see if they were startled by the thunder.

_____

_____

8 I calmed them down and dried them off in the backyard before I took them for a long walk.

_____

_____

9 By the time I finished walking the dogs they were tired and hungry, so I fed them before I left.

_____

_____

Traits of Good Writing • 6–8 © 2004 Creative Teaching Press

Rumors

FIRST/SECOND/THIRD PERSON

> Writing in the first person uses the first person pronoun, *I*. Writing in the second person uses the second person pronoun, *you*. Writing in the third person usually uses third person pronouns, such as *they, it, he,* or *she.*

Indicate if each statement matches the voice by writing a **C** if it is correct and an **I** if it is incorrect.

_____ **1** After breakfast, I took my little brother to school.   (first person)

_____ **2** You are wrong to repeat her secret to her classmates.   (third person)

_____ **3** They told her that the rumor that was going around school was about her parents.   (third person)

_____ **4** I don't blame her for being upset about the news.   (second person)

_____ **5** The teacher came in to speak to her after English period.   (third person)

_____ **6** She was confused about what was being said. (first person)

_____ **7** They didn't know how to respond. (second person)

_____ **8** The teacher helped to clear up the misunderstanding. (third person)

Rewrite each sentence from direct speech to indirect or reported speech.

9 Is Mr. Kim, our principal, planning to build a new basketball court?

_____

_____

10 I thought I saw her two brothers sneaking out of the neighbor's house with a bag.

_____

_____

11 Someone said, "Amanda's father is being relocated to a new office in Colorado so her family will be moving also."

_____

_____

Mr. Wolf

POINT OF VIEW

> The first person point of view is demonstrated when the author chooses one of the characters to tell the story. The reader can feel, act, and think along with the character, as the person tells the story.

Use a library to locate these two stories:
Three Little Pigs by Barry Moser (or any traditional version)
The True Story of the Three Little Pigs by Jon Scieszka (Viking, 1989)

Analyze the two stories and complete the blanks below.

Three Little Pigs
What's different?

❶ _____
❷ _____
❸ _____

The True Story of the Three Little Pigs
What's different?

❶ _____
❷ _____
❸ _____

What's common?

❶ _____
❷ _____
❸ _____

Based on the wolf's "true story," write a news report from his point of view.

The Wolf's Denial   by _____

"Good evening. This is Diane Watson on Channel 6 news with Mr. Black Wolf. He has a different view of the unfortunate destruction of the pigs' homes. Mr. Wolf?
"Thanks Diane. Hello. Everyone seems to think that I destroyed the three pigs' homes, but they are wrong. This is what really happened …

_____
_____
_____
_____
_____

Traits of Good Writing • 6–8 © 2004 Creative Teaching Press

What They Saw

POINT OF VIEW

The first-person point of view is demonstrated when the author chooses one of the characters to tell the story. The reader can feel, act, and think along with the character, as the person tells the story.

Write a first-person account of what each character saw, felt, and experienced in each scene.

The seven dwarves come home after a hard day in the mines and find that an intruder has broken into their home. They discover a beautiful lady asleep in their beds. Snow White awakes.

Snow White writes:

_____
_____
_____
_____

Grumpy writes:

_____
_____
_____
_____

The queen, disguised as an old peddler, approaches Snow White and gives her an apple. The dwarves have all gone to the mine to work. Snow White is cleaning house alone while her forest animal friends keep her company. They all know that the old woman is really the wicked queen. They try to warn and protect Snow White, but to no avail. Snow White takes a bite of the apple.

The wicked queen writes:

_____
_____
_____
_____

The forest animal friend, the rabbit, writes:

_____
_____
_____
_____

Traits of Good Writing • 6–8 © 2004 Creative Teaching Press

Ever After

POINT OF VIEW

> The first-person point of view is demonstrated when the author chooses one of the characters to tell the story. The reader can feel, act, and think along with the character, as the person tells the story.

Step into a fairy tale and try on the shoes of a different character. Write first-person accounts as if you were one of the characters.

Peter Pan is trying to save Wendy and her brothers from the evil Captain Hook. He is trapped on Captain Cook's ship, fighting for his life. The ship is full of confusion and screams as the pirates battle the brave rescuers. Soon the tide turns in the rescuers' favor and Captain Cook is defeated and eaten by the crocodile, Cook's enemy.

The crocodile gives an account of the final battle:

_____

_____

_____

_____

Cinderella is crying when her fairy godmother appears. Her godmother transforms a pumpkin, dogs, and mice into a horse-drawn carriage. Then she transforms poor ragged Cinderella into a lovely princess. Cinderella arrives at the ball and dances with the Prince until the clock strikes twelve.

Mouse shares his experience as a horse:

_____

_____

_____

_____

A stepsister's account of the ball:

_____

_____

_____

_____

Traits of Good Writing • 6–8 © 2004 Creative Teaching Press

Name _____ Date _____

Grocery List

DESCRIPTIVE WRITING

Getting the facts down on paper is one part of writing. Adding your voice to the piece creates interest for the reader.

Look at this grocery list. Choose three items from the list and describe them by adding your voice. Tell what your experience is with the items you choose and how you feel about them.

GROCERY LIST

Bread
Pizza dough
Orange juice
Oatmeal
Apples
Flour
Ice Cream

Grocery Item: _Oatmeal_
Oatmeal is a great breakfast on a cold, winter morning. But I only like it when I can add lots of brown sugar and a little bit of cream. Try to buy some that includes some sort of sweetener. Also, be sure to get the kind with individual packets. I like to take them with me when I go to my mom's for the weekend. They say oatmeal is "heart healthy." I don't know about that, but my taste buds seem to like it.

Grocery Item: _____
_____
_____
_____
_____
_____

Grocery Item: _____
_____
_____
_____
_____
_____

Grocery Item: _____
_____
_____
_____
_____

Traits of Good Writing • 6–8 © 2004 Creative Teaching Press

E-Voice

CONVEYING EMOTION

> For writing to be effective, there must be a connection between the reader and writer. An author can make this connection by showing emotion in his or her writing voice.

E-mails, because we often type them so quickly, are often void of any emotion. That is the reason we often add symbols, called emoticons, to help express our thoughts. Otherwise readers may wonder, "Is this person trying to tell me something? Is she mad?"

Express each thought in two ways—one in which you are happy and the other in which you are sad. Try using metaphors, similes, and analogies. Do not use the words *happy* and *sad*.

1 Monday is a holiday.
   Happy: <u>Sleeping in late, lounging around the house, and eating my favorite breakfast will be on my agenda this Monday!</u>
   Sad: <u>It stabs like a knife to know that I will not be going to school on Monday because I want desperately to see my friends.</u>

2 The tree was removed from the backyard on Saturday morning.
   Happy: _____
   _____
   Sad: _____
   _____

3 The principal retired and will not be coming back next year.
   Happy: _____
   _____
   Sad: _____
   _____

4 The mall opens at 8:00 a.m. this Sunday.
   Happy: _____
   _____
   Sad: _____
   _____

5 We sold the car to our neighbor for more than we expected.
   Happy: _____
   _____
   Sad: _____
   _____

Traits of Good Writing • 6–8 © 2004 Creative Teaching Press

Describe That Voice

IDENTIFYING VOICE

Read each passage. Use at least two different words to describe the voice in the piece. Do not use the same word twice.

1 I couldn't believe my eyes. Everything I'd worked for the entire year was scattered on the floor in a million pieces. I didn't know whether to laugh or cry. I think I did a little of both. Mostly I just stood still—very, very still.

_____

_____

2 My name was being repeated over the loudspeaker. Everyone in the room turned to look at me. I wasn't sure if I was physically getting smaller or if everyone else was growing freakishly large. I stood up and moved toward the door. It would take me a million years to walk that far when I was this tiny!

_____

_____

3 Looking in her eyes, I knew that no one would ever understand me this well. She had kept my biggest secret when it would have been so easy for her to tell everyone. I couldn't think of enough ways to say thank you. Fortunately, I was sure that she already understood.

_____

_____

4 My stomach hurt from laughing. If Billy made one more face or so much as looked sideways at me, I would lose it all over again. I watched the back of his red head, waiting for his next move. I felt the giggle explode from my throat as he spun around with a paper hat planted right on his nose!

_____

_____

Traits of Good Writing • 6–8 © 2004 Creative Teaching Press

Name _____ Date _____

If Voice Were...

Voice in writing reflects the very personal part of who you are. As a writer, you connect with your audience by sharing your unique, personal voice.

Read each question. Consider the personal items or ideas. Think about what they mean in your life. Then answer the question giving a specific example from your own experience.

Example: If voice were something in my room, what would it be?

If voice were something in my room, it would be my pillow because it fits perfectly under my arm when I sleep, it squishes to just the right size, and it smells like me.

1 If voice were a kind of food, what would it be?
_____
_____
_____

2 If voice were a subject in school, what would it be?
_____
_____
_____

3 If voice were a color, what would it be?
_____
_____
_____

4 If voice were a sound, what would it be?
_____
_____
_____

5 If voice were a smell, what would it be?
_____
_____
_____

Traits of Good Writing • 6–8 © 2004 Creative Teaching Press

Name _____ Date _____

Greeting Card Sentiments

> Greeting cards express sentiments or feelings in a concise way. They express a clear voice and emotion.

Write a greeting card message for each of the following kinds of cards. Use language that expresses the appropriate voice for each occasion.

1 Birthday Card

4 Condolence/Bereavement Card

2 New Job Card

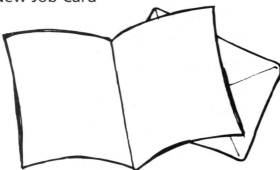

5 Get Well Card

3 New Baby Card

6 Humorous Friend Card

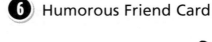

Using Your Voice

KNOWING YOUR AUDIENCE

Ultimately the thing that distinguishes you from every other writer is your voice. Voice is your personal way of telling a story. It includes how you think and how you feel. That is why authors create unique stories even if they begin with the same topic.

Imagine that you just received two tickets to Disneyland for your birthday.
Try using several different voices to communicate this information to different audiences.

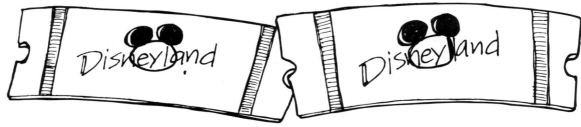

1 Tell your best friend.

_____

_____

2 Tell someone you are trying to impress.

_____

_____

3 Tell someone who went to Disneyland for his or her birthday.

_____

_____

4 Tell the President of the United States.

_____

_____

5 Tell your teacher (knowing you will need to miss a day of school to go).

_____

_____

6 Tell someone who has never heard of Disneyland.

_____

_____

7 Tell someone you plan to take with you with the second ticket.

_____

_____

Traits of Good Writing • 6–8 © 2004 Creative Teaching Press

Different Voices

Types of Voice

> Most forms of writing have a voice. A voice gives the reader a better understanding of what the author is trying to communicate. A voice reflects the author's personality, flavor, and style.

Can you recognize the voice in each passage? Label each passage using a word from the word box.

skeptical	scientific	excited	factual

1 That box was not there when I went to sleep! I bet it has my birthday present inside. I can't believe it! It looks like just the right size to be roller blades!

_____

2 Costa Rica is on the continent of North America. It is located on the narrow bridge of land at the southern end of North America that is called Central America.

_____

3 Well, I didn't hear about any random drawings or prizes. I think it might be a trick. What does the return address show?

_____

4 The food chain shows how all living things are connected to each other based on what they eat. Every link in the food chain is important.

_____

Write a sentence that expresses each type of voice.

5 anger

_____

_____

6 disappointment

_____

_____

7 humor

_____

_____

8 sarcasm

_____

_____

Traits of Good Writing • 6–8 © 2004 Creative Teaching Press

Whose Voice Is That?

IDENTIFYING VOICE

Each author tells a story in a unique way because each author filters information through his or her individual experience. You want your reader to have a picture of you by reading your work. Is this author young or old, thoughtful or bold, funny or sarcastic?

Write a sentence that expresses each type of voice.

1 bereaved

_____
_____

2 rude

_____
_____

3 frightened

_____
_____

4 zany

_____
_____

5 naïve

_____
_____

6 scholarly

_____
_____

7 superficial

_____
_____

8 sarcastic

_____
_____

Traits of Good Writing • 6–8 © 2004 Creative Teaching Press

Name _____ Date _____

Sleep and Dream

POETRY

Poetry is one way to express your own voice in writing. Beautiful language and flowing rhythms can combine to share feelings and emotions.
Haiku is one type of poem that uses expressive language in a concise but powerful way. A haiku has three lines and seventeen syllables. The first line has five syllables, the second line has seven syllables, and the third line has five syllables.

Drifting into sleep,
I fall, but not too deeply
A restful dreaming

Prepare to create your own haiku. Write three more subjects and then brainstorm some words for each category.

Subject	Adjectives	Verbs (participles, -ing, -ed)	Other nouns associated with the subject
1 sleep	deep restful	drift**ing** fall dream**ing**	pillow night
2 _____	_____ _____ _____	_____ _____ _____	_____ _____
3 _____	_____ _____ _____	_____ _____ _____	_____ _____
4 _____	_____ _____ _____	_____ _____ _____	_____ _____

Experiment with putting words together for the correct number of syllables per line.

_____
5 syllables

_____
7 syllables

_____
5 syllables

Traits of Good Writing • 6-8 © 2004 Creative Teaching Press

Name _____ Date _____

Spiders and Things

A **cinquain** is a short poem with five lines.

Spiders
Fuzzy, black
Hunting, creeping, spinning
Eight eyes glitter on head
Tarantulas

Prepare to create your own cinquain. Write three more subjects and then brainstorm some words for each category.

Subject	Adjectives	-ing Action Verbs	Other Names for Subject
❶ spiders	fuzzy black leggy	hunt**ing** creep**ing** spinn**ing**	tarantulas black widows
❷ _____	_____ _____ _____	_____ _____ _____	_____ _____
❸ _____	_____ _____ _____	_____ _____ _____	_____ _____
❹ _____	_____ _____ _____	_____ _____ _____	_____ _____

Write your own cinquain. Use words from your brainstorm notes to fill in the blanks. Start each line with a capital letter.

_____
subject

_____ , _____
adjective   adjective

_____ , _____ , _____
action word with –ing   action word with –ing   action word with –ing

_____
four- or five-word phrase about the subject

_____
another name for subject

Traits of Good Writing • 6–8 © 2004 Creative Teaching Press

Name _____ Date _____

Contrasts

POETRY

A **diamante poem** is a poem of seven lines in a diamond-shaped pattern that compares opposites.

Day
Light, lovely
Waking, rising, walking
Sunrise, pets, people, sunset
Sleeping, lying, stopping
Dark, silent
Night

Choose two more pairs of contrasting nouns. Brainstorm some words in each category.

Subject	Adjectives	Verbs (participles, -ing, -ed)	Nouns That Relate to the Subjects
1 Day Night	light, lovely dark, silent	waking, rising, walking sleeping, lying, stopping	sunrise, pets, people, sunset
2 _____ _____	_____ _____	_____ _____	_____ _____
3 _____ _____	_____ _____	_____ _____	_____ _____

Create your own diamante poem using words you have brainstormed.

_____
noun

_____, _____
2 adjectives that describe noun above

_____, _____, _____
3 verbs related to noun above

_____, _____, _____, _____
4 nouns related to both nouns

_____, _____, _____
3 verbs related to noun below

_____, _____
2 adjectives that describe noun below

_____
noun (opposite of line 1)

Traits of Good Writing • 6–8 © 2004 Creative Teaching Press

Familiar or Foreign?

FOREIGN WORDS

Using words and phrases derived from other languages can add interest to your writing and help its flow.

Using context clues, choose the best definition for each foreign word or phrase. Circle your answer.

1 bona fide (boh'na fide) Latin
Even though she displayed extreme modesty, it was clear that she was a bona fide expert in her field.
   a. skeptical
   b. genuine
   c. rude

2 carpe diem (kar'pay dee'um) Latin
So what if you have a 7:30 a.m. class tomorrow and a full afternoon of basketball practice? Carpe diem!
   a. get some sleep
   b. cancel your appointments
   c. seize the day

3 caveat emptor (kav'ee-ot emp'tor) Latin
Before you leap at that real estate deal, caveat emptor!
   a. call your lawyer
   b. let the buyer beware
   c. count your money

4 faux pas (foh pah') French
Miss Bryant was embarrassed to realize she had unwittingly committed yet another faux pas.
   a. social blunder
   b. felony
   c. assignment

5 je ne sais quoi (zhun say kwah') French
He had a certain unexplainable je ne sais quoi that she found intriguing.
   a. elusive quality
   b. amount of money
   c. speech impediment

6 savoir-faire (sav'wahr fair') French
She conducted the meeting with an impressive savoir-faire.
   a. loud voice
   b. video presentation
   c. ability to say and do the correct thing

7 mano a mano (mah'no ah mah'no) Spanish
Please leave me alone. I want to handle this guy mano a mano.
   a. in the alley
   b. face-to-face in a confrontation
   c. tomorrow

8 ad nauseam (ad noz'ee-um) Latin
The teacher shouted directions one after another ad nauseam.
   a. to a sickening degree
   b. softly
   c. angrily

Traits of Good Writing • 6–8 © 2004 Creative Teaching Press

Heads and Tails

PREFIXES

> Increasing your vocabulary will give you new word choices to use when you write. Knowing the meaning of prefixes can help you decipher the meaning of new words.

Complete the words by adding a prefix from the word box to each word part. Then match each new word to its definition by writing a letter on each blank.

| sub- (under) | mono- (one) | circum- (around) | inter- (between) |
| super- (over) | bi- (two) | trans- (across) | intra- (within) |

_____ **1** _____tone

_____ **2** _____monthly

_____ **3** _____cutaneous

_____ **4** _____impose

_____ **5** _____personal

_____ **6** _____mural

_____ **7** _____ference

_____ **8** _____atlantic

A. across the Atlantic Ocean
B. to lay or place something over something else
C. the distance around a circle
D. speech in which every word has one tone or voice
E. between two people
F. happening every two months
G. involving students from within the same school
H. under the skin

Write a definition for each word. Use the meaning of each prefix to help you.

9 transport _____

10 intragalactic _____

11 interject _____

12 subconscious _____

13 biennial _____

14 monorail _____

Suffix Sense

SUFFIXES

A **suffix** is a word part added to the end of a word. A root or base word plus a suffix creates a new word with a new meaning.

Complete the words by adding a suffix from the word box to each word part. Then match each new word to its definition by writing a letter on each blank.

| -ful (full of) | -ward (moving to) | -less (without) | -able, -ible (able to) |
| -ist (one who practices) | -ly (like) | -ment (act, condition of) | -er, -or (doer) |

_____ **1** doubt _____
_____ **2** pian _____
_____ **3** neighbor _____
_____ **4** content _____
_____ **5** back _____
_____ **6** ed _____
_____ **7** blame _____
_____ **8** act _____

A. one who practices piano
B. moving back
C. without blame
D. like a neighbor
E. one who acts
F. condition of being content
G. full of doubt
H. able to be eaten

Write a definition for each word. Then use the word in a sentence.

9 accessible _____
_____

10 juror _____
_____

11 geologist _____
_____

12 disappointment _____
_____

Traits of Good Writing • 6–8 © 2004 Creative Teaching Press

Name _____ Date _____

Verb Makeover

LIVELY VERBS

> **Verbs** are action words that describe actions or states of being. Choosing colorful verbs will add more sparkle to your writing.

Cross out the verb(s) in each sentence and replace it with a more lively, interesting verb. Rewrite the sentence using the new verb choice.

1 The train moved over the mountain pass.

_____

2 The wood burned in the fire.

_____

3 The soda spilled from the shaken can.

_____

4 The car slid on the icy patch of road.

_____

5 The leaves blew along the dirt path.

_____

Some verbs are tired and overused. Thinking of more interesting and lively substitutes for those words will improve the quality of your writing. Write five alternatives for each of these overused verbs. Be creative.

said	walked	cried	slept

Traits of Good Writing • 6-8 © 2004 Creative Teaching Press

Don't Just Sit There!

ACTIVE AND PASSIVE VERBS

> The subject of an active sentence <u>performs</u> the action of the verb.
> **The dog bit the boy.**
> The subject of a passive sentence just sits there, <u>receiving</u> it.
> **The boy was bitten by the dog.**
> Using active verbs will make your writing more dynamic and give it more life.

Determine if each sentence uses an active or a passive verb. Write **A** if the verb is active or **P** if it is passive.

_____ **1** The book is being read by most of the class.

_____ **2** Over one-third of the students failed the exam.

_____ **3** Her brakes were slammed on when she saw the red light.

_____ **4** Action on the proposal is being considered by the PTA committee.

_____ **5** The surgeons performed the experimental surgery successfully.

_____ **6** Worried store owners are seeking a fair compromise to end the strike.

_____ **7** The new policy was approved by the school board.

_____ **8** An excellent score was given to the novice musician by the judge.

_____ **9** The coach threw the ball into the dugout.

_____ **10** I learned how to juggle in just two days!

Use an active verb to rewrite each sentence above that has a passive verb.

11 _____

12 _____

13 _____

14 _____

15 _____

Traits of Good Writing • 6–8 © 2004 Creative Teaching Press

Name _____ Date _____

First Day

Adjectives

> **Adjectives** are words that describe nouns or pronouns. The degrees of comparison are known as the positive, the comparative, and the superlative. The **comparative** form is used to compare two nouns or pronouns. The **superlative** form is used to compare three or more.

Write the correct form of each adjective.

Positive	Comparative	Superlative
1 clean	_____	_____
2 colorful	_____	_____
3 strong	_____	_____
4 green	_____	_____
5 disruptive	_____	_____
6 secure	_____	_____
7 healthy	_____	_____
8 lovely	_____	_____
9 terrifying	_____	_____
10 talkative	_____	_____

Use an adjective from above to complete each sentence.

11 Welcome to South Lane High, Mrs. Daniels. We are proud of our school and we try very hard to maintain a _____ environment here.

12 In case you have not noticed, we have the _____ school grounds in the district.

13 Yes, I was just commenting how much _____ the grass is here. These azaleas and hydrangeas make this entrance _____ and pleasing to the eye.

14 It is _____ in summer than in fall, when the flowers are in full bloom.

15 We have higher standards, and, therefore, a _____ program and staff here than at your former school.

Adding Details

Adverbs

Adverbs modify verbs, adjectives, or other adverbs. When answering the question *how?*, adverbs are usually created from adjectives with an added -ly ending. Adverbs can also answer the questions *where?*, *when?*, and *how often?*

She spoke **quickly.** (how)
She spoke **here.** (where)
She spoke **yesterday.** (when)
She spoke **every day.** (how often)

Underline the verb and circle the adverb in each sentence. Choose a word from the word box to tell what question the adverb answers. Write it on the line.

how	where	when	how often

1. That woman lives upstairs. _____

2. He calls his mother often. _____

3. The senator ran swiftly to catch the bus. _____

4. The mouse moved slowly. _____

5. Please leave your coat here. _____

6. The chicks were eagerly pecking at the birdseed in the yard. _____

7. She tries to return before dark. _____

8. The seamstress quickly made the skirt. _____

9. The woman in the red dress finished her tea first. _____

10. She takes the boat to the mainland every day. _____

11. An eagle soared above. _____

12. Beth works enthusiastically. _____

13. The dogs barked fiercely at the stranger. _____

14. I know you are waiting patiently for your friend to arrive. _____

15. The old cat naps frequently. _____

16. Class, please listen to the question carefully. _____

Traits of Good Writing • 6–8 © 2004 Creative Teaching Press

Storm Warning

ADVERBS

Adverbs can be written in comparison forms—positive, comparative, and superlative.

Complete the chart by adding the missing forms of each adverb.

Positive	Comparative	Superlative
fast	faster	fastest
1 clear	_____	_____
2 _____	more transparent	_____
3 quick	_____	_____
4 decisive	_____	_____
5 far	_____	_____

Circle the adverbs in each sentence.

6 Suddenly, the lifeguard noticed a woman yelling hysterically. Her eight-year-old son was missing and he was last seen splashing merrily in the waves.

7 Immediately, the lifeguard grabbed his flotation device firmly and ran speedily down the beach.

8 The woman spotted a boy bobbing nearby. Running quickly to the lifeguard, she breathlessly spoke and pointed vaguely to where she briefly saw her son.

Write the correct form of each adverb.

9 The surfers and swimmers heard the warning that the typhoon was approaching _____ (comparative form of *quick*) than the meteorologist had anticipated.

10 The warning came suddenly. Typhoons were rare in summer here. This typhoon was also traveling _____ (comparative form of *erratic*) than the other typhoons this season.

11 The lifeguards worked _____ (positive form of *decisive*). They continued to evacuate the beach _____ (positive form of *urgent*), working _____ (positive form of *consistent*) from one end of the beach to the other.

Traits of Good Writing • 6–8 © 2004 Creative Teaching Press

Name _____ Date _____

Moving to the City

ADVERBS AND ADJECTIVES

> **Adjectives** are words that describe nouns or pronouns. The adjectives may be in the positive, comparative, or superlative form.
> **Adverbs** are words that modify actions or verbs. They answer the questions *where?, when?, how often?,* and *how?* Many adverbs end in -ly.
> Improve your sentences by using more specific or stronger adjectives and adverbs.

Circle a word to replace the underlined word to make a stronger statement.

1 Catherine, who is a New York executive, lives a <u>busy</u> life in the city.
  a. quick   **b.** hectic   **c.** busiest

2 The office secretary, Mrs. Lim, is a(n) <u>good</u> worker. She usually gets her work done on time.
  a. efficient   **b.** helpful   **c.** timely

3 When the young eaglet heard its mother's <u>sharp</u> voice, it looked up.
  a. shouting   **b.** shrieking   **c.** loud

4 They are going to visit their aunt, whose house is next to a <u>flowing</u> brook.
  a. rippling   **b.** singing   **c.** bubbly

Use a word from the word box to complete each sentence.

anxiously	disastrous	refreshing	reluctantly
annoying	exhausted	dawn	wearily

5 She hoped that moving to the city would go more smoothly than her last, rather _____ move.
  (difficult)

6 The _____ alarm rang at _____. Cathy was
  (unpleasant)   (early)

_____ but awake.
  (tired)

7 She took a _____ shower and _____ dressed, while waiting
  (nice)   (tiredly)

_____ for the moving van and her friends to arrive.
  (worriedly)

8 Ben, Jim, and Don had agreed _____ to help her move today.
  (with hesitation)

Traits of Good Writing • 6-8 © 2004 Creative Teaching Press

Join 'Em Up

CONJUNCTIONS

A **conjunction** is a joiner—a word that connects (conjoins) parts of a sentence. **Subordinating conjunctions** help to show cause-effect relationships. Subordinating conjunctions join two clauses, making one clause dependent (or subordinate) upon the other. A subordinating conjunction may appear at the beginning of a sentence or between the two clauses.

It is raining. + We have an umbrella. = Because it is raining, we have an umbrella.

Use a subordinating conjunction from the word box to join each pair of sentences. Write each new sentence on the line.

even though	now that	whenever	so that
because	rather than	whereas	

1 The tropical forest is very damp. The rainfall has been light this year.

_____

2 The two friends became more cautious. They narrowly escaped the tiger.

_____

3 You finished painting the room. The makeover is complete.

_____

4 Justin stood up. The young child had a place to sit.

_____

5 Mrs. Pak bakes cookies. The entire neighborhood stops by for a sample.

_____

6 She did not join her friends at the party. She decided to go home.

_____

7 Britney chose to attend college. Her mother did not have the same opportunity.

_____

Traits of Good Writing • 6–8 © 2004 Creative Teaching Press

Name _____ Date _____

Think Again

REPLACING OVERUSED WORDS

When you write, use the most precise word for your meaning, not the word that comes to mind first. If you need help, remember you can use a thesaurus to find alternatives for commonly overused words.

Use a word from the word box to replace the underlined overused word in each sentence. Rewrite each sentence.

tolerate	tremendous	conceive	defective
receive	pleasant	formidable	comprehend

1 I realized when I got home and opened the box that the remote control was <u>bad.</u>

_____

2 Phillip claimed that because he did not <u>know</u> the rule he was unable to abide by it.

_____

3 While on the boat cruise, we noticed a <u>big</u> whale flipping its tail in the water.

_____

4 We enjoyed a <u>nice</u> afternoon in Mrs. Hetzel's summer garden.

_____

5 The family could not <u>take</u> the hot weather any longer so they moved to Minnesota.

_____

6 The new student could not even <u>think</u> of cheating on the test.

_____

7 The high school senior was anxious to <u>get</u> his diploma.

_____

8 The prize was tempting, but the stunt was too <u>hard.</u>

_____

Traits of Good Writing • 6–8 © 2004 Creative Teaching Press

Name _____ Date _____

Off Limits

DESCRIPTIVE WRITING

Sometimes we use the same words over and over, making our writing boring and predictable. Using rich, colorful words can paint a picture in the reader's mind. Make an effort to try new words. Use a thesaurus if you need help.

Write a paragraph telling about each topic described below. Be careful not to use any of the "off limits" words listed for each topic.

Topic #1: Write about a victory.

Off Limits! excited, embarrassed, thrilled, happy, great

_____
_____
_____
_____
_____

Topic #2: Write about a skill you learned.

Off Limits! frustrated, hard, easy, interesting

_____
_____
_____
_____

Topic #3: Write about losing something.

Off Limits! looked, wonder, sad, happy

_____
_____
_____
_____
_____

Topic #4: Write a description of a friend.

Off Limits! nice, good, sweet, kind, cool

_____
_____
_____
_____
_____

Traits of Good Writing • 6–8 © 2004 Creative Teaching Press

Similar To . . .

SIMILES

A **simile** is used to compare two things, often using the word *like* or *as.* Using similes can help you create a word picture for the reader.

1 Underline the phrases that are similes.

changeable as the weather	deceptive snake	silent as the grave
a brave lion	brave as a lion	you stubborn mule
deceptive as a snake	a red, red rose	lovely as a rose
cool cucumbers	quick as lightning	bright as day

Brainstorm a list of items that can be compared to the underlined word in each sentence. Then use one of them to create a simile. Rewrite each sentence using the new comparison.

2 She can run <u>fast.</u>
Things that are fast: cheetah, race car, sprinter
Sentence rewrite: _____

3 The breeze was <u>light and airy.</u>
Things that are light and airy: _____
Sentence rewrite: _____

4 The sky was <u>dark.</u>
Things that are dark: _____
Sentence rewrite: _____

5 The night was <u>quiet.</u>
Things that are quiet: _____
Sentence rewrite: _____

6 The blanket was <u>soft.</u>
Things that are soft: _____
Sentence rewrite: _____

7 The flower was <u>delicate.</u>
Things that are delicate: _____
Sentence rewrite: _____

Traits of Good Writing • 6–8 © 2004 Creative Teaching Press

Create a Mental Picture

METAPHORS

A **metaphor** is a figure of speech that compares unlike things by saying that one thing is the other. Metaphors allow you to create a mental picture for your reader using a minimum of words.

Describe each noun using a metaphoric comparison. Then create a list of interpretations your reader may infer from your comparison.

1 Bedroom
Metaphor: _My bedroom is a prison._____
Interpretation: _The bedroom is small and cramped. The bedroom's owner may feel deprived_
_and lonely._____

2 Garden
Metaphor: _____
Interpretation: _____
_____

3 School
Metaphor: _____
Interpretation: _____
_____

4 Theater
Metaphor: _____
Interpretation: _____
_____

5 Flower
Metaphor: _____
Interpretation: _____
_____

6 Hamburger
Metaphor: _____
Interpretation: _____
_____

As Big as a Barn

Hyperbole

Hyperbole is a type of figurative language. Sometimes it is confused with simile or metaphor because it often compares two objects. The difference is a hyperbole is an exaggeration. Hyperbole often uses humor as well.

Here are some examples of hyperbole:

I nearly died laughing.
I tried a thousand times.
He's as big as a house.

I'm so hungry I could eat a horse.
I could sleep for a year.
This book weighs a ton.

Create your own examples of hyperbole using these sentence starters.

1 My sister uses so much makeup that _____
_____

2 My dog is so cute _____
_____

3 My hometown is so small you could _____
_____

4 His feet were so big _____
_____

5 That student is so lazy he _____
_____

6 The class was so boring we _____
_____

7 This homework assignment is so hard _____
_____

Traits of Good Writing • 6–8 © 2004 Creative Teaching Press

What Are You Saying?

IDIOMS

An **idiom** is an expression that has a meaning apart from the meaning of its individual words. When we say, "It's raining cats and dogs," we don't literally mean that cats and dogs are falling from the sky. The phrase suggests that it is raining very hard.

Match each idiom with its meaning.

_____ **1** cream of the crop

_____ **2** blue in the face

_____ **3** eager beaver

_____ **4** hard nut to crack

_____ **5** badger someone

_____ **6** bull in a china shop

_____ **7** cut off your nose to spite your face

_____ **8** cat's got your tongue

_____ **9** half-baked

_____ **10** bark up the wrong tree

_____ **11** keep your nose out of it

_____ **12** black and white

_____ **13** horse of a different color

_____ **14** hit between the eyes

A. get someone to do something by repeated questions or by bothering him or her

B. a person with no tact who upsets others or upsets plans

C. choose the wrong course of action

D. can't speak because of shyness

E. a person who is always eager to work or do something extra

F. make a strong impression on; surprise greatly

G. best of a group; the top choice

H. not thought out or studied carefully

I. thinking of everything or judging everything as either good or bad

J. something difficult to do or someone hard to understand

K. very angry or upset, excited, and very emotional

L. something totally separate and different

M. make things worse for yourself because you are angry

N. keep out of or away from

Write three sentences using three of the idioms from above.

15 _____

_____

16 _____

_____

17 _____

_____

Make the Connections

An **analogy** is a comparison that takes the form "A is to B as C is to D." The relationship of A and B is compared to the relationship of C and D. From this simple form of an analogy, you will notice the most important thing—its parallel construction.

Use the word choices provided to complete each analogy. Circle your answer.

1. car is to engine as wing is to ____   crocodile   plane   pilot

2. petal is to daisy as needle is to ____   pine   maple   grass

3. grip is to fingers as bow is to ____   waist   ankle   mouth

4. plummer is to wrench as musician is to ____ music   instrument song

5. digestion is to stomach as respiration is to ____ lungs   fins   mouth

6. track is to train as runway is to ____   airplane   bicycle   athlete

7. courtesy is to attention as rudeness is to ____ exclamation interruption prediction

8. tomorrow is to today as ____ is to current futuristic   predictable timing

9. designer is to artistic as author is to ____ literary   conducive   journal

10. loser is to victory as winner is to ____   win   defeat   qualification

11. car is to steer as ship is to ____   drive   captain   navigate

12. orange is to rind as candy is to ____   wrapper   seeds   juice

13. agreement is to harmony as conflict is to ____ suspicion dischord emotion

The next step . . .
Making the analogy parallel is the first and easiest step in making an analogy. The second step is a bit trickier.

Shoes are to running as pens are to writing

This comparison, of writing to running, might seem at first to be useless. However, if we were composing an advertisement for writing instruments to be placed in a running magazine, it might be helpful to convince runners that a good pen is as important to writing as good shoes are to running.

Traits of Good Writing • 6–8 © 2004 Creative Teaching Press

Name _____ Date _____

Same Difference

SYNONYMS

> **Synonyms** are words that have the same or similar meanings.

Circle the word that is a synonym for the underlined word in each sentence.

1 The guests received <u>free</u> access to all areas of the sound stage.
   a. unrestricted
   b. limited
   c. important
   d. exclusive

2 His <u>inquisitive</u> nature prompted a plethora of questions about the movie.
   a. happy
   b. determined
   c. inquiring
   d. outgoing

3 The <u>obscure</u> reference made the example difficult to understand.
   a. easy
   b. ambiguous
   c. fancy
   d. annoying

4 The concept of forgiveness was <u>prevalent</u> among the jurors.
   a. widespread
   b. unacceptable
   c. missing
   d. lost

5 Carla made an attempt to <u>transform</u> the timid girl into a confident young woman.
   a. retain
   b. mislead
   c. rewrite
   d. convert

6 The <u>blunder</u> was overlooked by the judge.
   a. mistake
   b. question
   c. answer
   d. conclusion

7 After watching the fast-paced action movie, the historical biography seemed <u>dull</u> by comparison.
   a. exciting
   b. lackluster
   c. humorous
   d. outrageous

8 The young soldier approached his assignment with <u>courage</u> and determination.
   a. fearlessness
   b. anxiety
   c. carelessness
   d. pride

9 An attempt to <u>mask</u> the evidence was impossible when the facts were so compelling.
   a. harden
   b. relax
   c. conceal
   d. command

10 The prisoner was <u>released</u> after the sentence was served.
   a. discharged
   b. beaten
   c. ambushed
   d. interrogated

Traits of Good Writing • 6-8 © 2004 Creative Teaching Press

Think Opposite

ANTONYMS

Antonyms are words with opposite meanings.

Match each word with its antonym in the word box. Write the word on the line.

cowardly	life	deficient	doubt	acknowledge
mitigate	surrender	conclusion	grotesque	unique
incompetent	artificial	inattentive	brash	

1 courageous _____

2 ignore _____

3 sufficient _____

4 believe _____

5 common _____

6 natural _____

7 overcome _____

8 beginning _____

9 beautiful _____

10 alert _____

11 aggravate _____

12 death _____

13 able _____

14 shy _____

Create antonyms using a prefix or suffix from the word box.

il-	un-	ir-	in-	dis-	im-	-less	-ful

15 harmful   harm_____

16 legal   _____legal

17 lodge   _____lodge

18 regular   _____regular

19 just   _____just

20 joyful   joy_____

21 articulate   _____articulate

22 responsible   _____responsible

23 restless   rest_____

24 discreet   _____discreet

25 cheerless   cheer_____

26 obedient   _____obedient

27 productive   _____productive

28 thoughtful   thought_____

Traits of Good Writing • 6–8 © 2004 Creative Teaching Press

How Does the Word Make You Feel?

CONNOTATION

The relationship between words and meanings can be quite complicated. Words do not always have single, simple meanings. The **denotation** of a word is its literal meaning. The **connotation** is the association a word has in our minds.
All three underlined words have a similar denotation but they each evoke a different connotation.
I am <u>selective</u>.   You are <u>choosy</u>.   She is <u>fussy</u>.

Look at each pair of words. One creates a more negative connotation while the other is more positive. Identify the one that has the most positive connotation in your mind by writing a **P** beside it.

1 _____ thinking   _____ daydreaming

2 _____ dancing   _____ jiggling about

3 _____ smirking   _____ smiling

4 _____ sniveling   _____ weeping

5 _____ writing   _____ scribbling

6 _____ energetic   _____ jumpy

7 _____ conceited   _____ confident

talking or babbling?

When writing a persuasive piece, remember to select words that evoke a connotation that will increase your persuasiveness. Choose two pairs of words from above and write a sentence using each word that appropriately fits the connotation each word evokes.

8 Word Pair: _____ and _____

Sentence #1 _____

Sentence #2 _____

9 Word Pair: _____ and _____

Sentence #1 _____

Sentence #2 _____

Name _____ Date _____

Crickety, Creak

ONOMATOPOEIA

> **Onomatopoeia** is the use of words, such as *buzz* or *purr*, that imitate the sounds associated with the objects or actions they refer to. Using onomatopoeia can add rhythm and fluency to your writing.

Circle the words that represent onomatopoeia in each sentence.

1 The young woman sat quietly listening to the rhythmic tick-tock of the grandfather clock as each minute slowly passed.

2 Crickety, creak! The old chair groaned with every movement I made.

3 With a swishing of its tail, the black cat disappeared into the smoke.

4 When the wolf started to howl, Danny's puppy yelped.

5 The burning wood crackled and hissed as the embers sailed away into the night air.

6 The moving truck creaked forward as the old engine began to sputter.

Use words from the word box to add onomatopoeia to each sentence.

splat	swish	splash	squeaking	boom	quacking

7 "Why wait my friend? It is my time to go." With a loud _____of his heavy cloak, the magician grinned and disappeared.

8 The egg landed on the floor with a _____ as the frantic chef tried to quickly scramble up a breakfast dish.

9 The young girl walked across the room while her classmates giggled at the _____ coming from her shoes.

10 The loud _____ sounded like it was coming from the attic.

11 The whale made a huge _____ when its tail swatted the water.

12 The constant _____ of the mallards reminded us that we were no longer in the city.

Traits of Good Writing • 6–8 © 2004 Creative Teaching Press

Sweet Smell of Success

ALLITERATION

Alliteration is the repetition of the same consonant sound at the beginning of words used in a phrase or sentence, such as "I hope I **w**in the **w**acky **w**eekend at **W**averly **W**aves!" Alliteration is fun to say and enjoyable to hear. Using alliteration can add rhythm and fluency to your writing.

1 Alliteration is often used in clichés. Circle the clichés that use alliteration.

give and take
sweet smell of success
out on a limb
taken for a ride
a dime a dozen
that's the ticket

jump for joy
lay of the land
wish upon a star
as good as gold
clean bill of health
bigger and better

Create your own alliterative phrases.

2 **M** Use two words that begin with the letter **m.**

_____

3 **P** Use two words that begin with the letter **p.**

_____

4 **T** Use four words that begin with the letter **t.**

_____

5 **R** Use three words that begin with the letter **r.**

_____

6 **S** Use three words that begin with the letter **s.**

_____

Traits of Good Writing • 6–8 © 2004 Creative Teaching Press

Name _____ Date _____

Sensory Scene

SENSORY WORDS

Sensory words relate to our five senses. They describe the way a subject or object looks, smells, sounds, tastes, or feels.

Write descriptive phrases that help the reader see, smell, hear, taste, and feel what you sense by looking at the scene above.

Briefcase

look   expensive and leathery

smell   gives off a warm, rich scent

sound   _____

feel   as smooth as silk

Donuts

look   _____

smell   _____

taste   _____

feel   _____

Dog

look   _____

smell   _____

sound   _____

feel   _____

Newspapers

look   _____

smell   _____

sound   _____

feel   _____

Choose one set of descriptive phrases and use as many as you can to write an artfully crafted descriptive sentence.

_____

_____

Traits of Good Writing • 6–8 © 2004 Creative Teaching Press

Off to a Good Start

SENTENCE BEGINNINGS

Good writing includes sentences that begin in different ways. If the sentences in a passage or story all begin the same way, the writing can become boring. Remember to use a variety of sentence beginnings.

Use each starter to create a sentence.

1 In the morning, _____.

2 Yesterday _____.

3 I never knew _____.

4 Though most students do not, _____.

5 If you have _____.

Rearrange the words in each sentence to give it a different beginning. Change just the order of the words, not the meaning of the sentence.

6 I watched the train pass by slowly as the wind began to howl.

As the wind began to howl, I watched the train pass by slowly._____

7 Jeremy inhaled the pizza before his sister could have one bite.

_____

8 While making our way to the summit, it began to snow.

_____

9 My homework assignment fell into the mud before I realized I had even dropped my book.

_____

10 They were surprised to see a good selection of CDs left since it was already Friday.

_____

Name _____ Date _____

Sentence Sense

COMPLETE/INCOMPLETE SENTENCES

> A **complete sentence** contains at least one subject and one verb.
> An **incomplete sentence** is missing a subject and/or verb. Clauses and phrases are incomplete sentences.

Use the phrases to make complete sentences. Be sure you include a subject and a verb.

1 hot and spicy tacos

_____

2 stand in line

_____

3 warm delicious breakfast

_____

4 today's menu

_____

Use a word from the word box to complete each sentence.

lines	lunch bell	table	selection	geography
effort	friends	cafeteria	Jenny	stomachs

Lunch came after the (5)_____ period. John, Jenny, and Maggie could not

wait for the break, for their (6)_____ were starting to growl hungrily.

Finally, the (7)_____ rang! The hungry (8)_____ ran immediately

to the (9)_____ in an (10)_____ to beat the (11)_____.

(12)_____ went to save a (13)_____, while the others stood in line

and read today's menu. They were surprised to see a good (14)_____.

Traits of Good Writing • 6–8 © 2004 Creative Teaching Press

Name _____ Date _____

Clause Connection

INDEPENDENT/DEPENDENT CLAUSES

A **clause** consists of a subject and a verb (unlike a phrase). A clause can be independent or dependent.

Independent clause: a group of words that contains a subject and verb and expresses a complete thought

Dependent clause: a group of words that contains a subject and verb but does not express a complete thought (a dependent clause cannot be a sentence)

Identify each clause as independent **(I)** or dependent **(D)**.

_____ **1** wherever there are computers

_____ **2** we will go eat after the show is over

_____ **3** she received the assignment

_____ **4** so that she would win the contest

_____ **5** Because Lisa was laughing at the joke

_____ **6** today is Tuesday

_____ **7** our papers are due on Wednesday

_____ **8** if you save your money

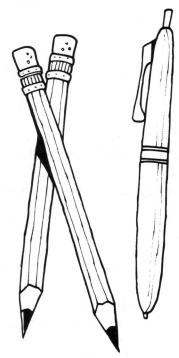

Use each dependent clause from 1–8 to write a complete sentence.

9 _____

_____

10 _____

_____

11 _____

_____

12 _____

_____

Enjoy!

SENTENCE COMBINING

Sentence combining is a great tool to create longer, more interesting sentences from several shorter, choppy ones. It also helps if you sprinkle in some adjectives to enhance the sensory experience.

Combine each set of short, choppy sentences into one sentence. Add at least one new adjective to your new sentence.

1 Bonnie had lunch at the Chinese Garden restaurant.
Bonnie ate noodles.
She drank tea.

_____

_____

_____

2 Everyone received an invitation.
They all went to the party.
The Mayor's Ball was a grand event.

_____

_____

_____

3 Ellen wore a hat.
She wore a warm winter coat.
She left her house.
She went to the concert.

_____

_____

_____

4 The zookeeper awakes at dawn.
He makes sure all the animals are fed.
He checks to be sure the cages are clean.

_____

_____

_____

Traits of Good Writing • 6–8 © 2004 Creative Teaching Press

Name _____ Date _____

Sentence Secrets

SIMPLE/COMPOUND/COMPLEX SENTENCES

> One of the secrets to fluent writing is to use various types of sentence structures. This can add variety to your writing and help hold the reader's interest.

Simple sentence: independent clause with one subject and verb pair
Compound sentence: two or more simple sentences joined by a conjunction, a semicolon, or a comma
Complex sentence: combination of an independent clause and a dependent clause

Underline the subject and circle the verb in each sentence.

1 Getting enough sleep may improve your memory.

2 Hawaii is known for macadamia nuts and Kona coffee.

3 Course salt sprinkled on pretzels delivers a burst of flavor.

4 Spring brings warmer temperatures and longer days.

5 Buyers whose remotes don't control the TV, may upgrade to the new all-in-one remote.

Identify each sentence type. Circle your answer.

6 Don't leave your bike out in the rain; it will get rusty.
      simple   compound   complex

7 Please help your sister with her homework.
      simple   compound   complex

8 Because the dog begged so fervently, the student couldn't eat his pizza.
      simple   compound   complex

9 Julia and Stephanie are working together on a science project.
      simple   compound   complex

10 Did you find my math book in my locker, or was it on the kitchen table?
      simple   compound   complex

Traits of Good Writing • 6–8 © 2004 Creative Teaching Press

Name _____   Date _____

Ball. Ball? Ball!

SENTENCE TYPES

Using the correct type of sentence and punctuating it correctly can add more interest to your writing.

Imperative sentence: Makes a request or gives a command
Interrogative sentence: Asks a question
Declarative sentence: Provides information
Exclamatory sentence: Expresses strong feelings or emotions

Identify each type of sentence and provide the correct ending punctuation.

_____ **1** Why do soccer balls have multi-colored panels____

_____ **2** I can't believe the ball burst when the player took a penalty kick____

_____ **3** Who has the game ball____

_____ **4** A soccer ball can weigh no more than 16 ounces____

_____ **5** It must be a thrill to make it to the big leagues____

_____ **6** You can't play the game if you don't know the rules____

_____ **7** Do not go out of bounds or the play will not count____

_____ **8** Who makes the rules____

_____ **9** Do not cheer when the other team has made a mistake____

_____ **10** Never criticize the referee____

_____ **11** We won our first game____

_____ **12** Dribbling the ball around the field is a good warm-up exercise__

Write a short paragraph. Use each type of sentence at least once.

_____

_____

_____

_____

Traits of Good Writing • 6–8 © 2004 Creative Teaching Press

Name _____ Date _____

Newspaper Search

Sentence Variety

> Newspaper reporters must make sense of the information they receive. In some cases, they need to restate questions. Other times they quote answers. Reporters use different kinds of sentences to make their articles flow.

Use a newspaper to find two examples of each kind of sentence. Then write your own sentence for each category.

Declarative

1 _____

2 _____

3 _____

Imperative

4 _____

5 _____

6 _____

Interrogative

7 _____

8 _____

9 _____

Exclamatory

10 _____

11 _____

12 _____

Traits of Good Writing • 6–8 © 2004 Creative Teaching Press

Create and Combine

SENTENCE LENGTH

> Short, choppy sentences can inhibit the flow of your writing. Often these short sentences can be combined using transitional words, descriptive phrases, clauses, and more complex sentence structures.

Read each set of short sentences. Combine them into one fluid sentence that still conveys the same meaning.

Set #1
We went to the park.
It was a sunny day.
We ate a picnic lunch.

_____

_____

Set #2
He washed his car.
It looked shiny.
He was tired when he finished.

_____

_____

Set #3
Elizabeth baked cookies.
They smelled delicious.
Everyone wanted to try one.

_____

_____

Set #4
I learned to ski.
It was scary at first.
I am proud of my accomplishment.

_____

_____

Traits of Good Writing • 6–8 © 2004 Creative Teaching Press

Mix It Up

VARIED SENTENCE STRUCTURE

How sentences sound to your ear depends greatly on their structure. If all of your sentences are structured the same, your writing will lack interest and sound choppy. One way to vary sentence structure is to end sentences with different parts of speech.

The proof is in the <u>pudding.</u> (noun ending)
In the pudding the proof can be <u>found.</u> (verb ending)
If you are looking for the proof, the pudding is where you will find <u>it.</u> (pronoun ending)

Rewrite each sentence so it ends with the part of speech indicated.

1 Don't count your chickens before they hatch.
(pronoun) _____

2 All work and no play makes Jack a dull boy.
(adjective) _____

3 When the cat's away, the mice will play.
(noun) _____

4 An apple a day keeps the doctor away.
(verb) _____

5 Better to die with honor than live with shame.
(verb) _____

6 There is more than one way to skin a cat.
(pronoun) _____

7 Those who live in glass houses should not throw stones.
(verb) _____

8 All is fair in love and war.
(adjective) _____

9 Don't put all your eggs in one basket.
(pronoun) _____

10 The grass is always greener on the other side of the fence.
(adjective) _____

Good for Glue

Transitional Words

Transitional words and phrases provide the glue that holds ideas together in writing. Using transitional words and phrases provides coherence, which creates writing that is smooth to read.

Choose the best transitional word or phrase from the glue bottle to complete each sentence.

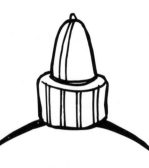

furthermore

at the same time

meanwhile

similarly

consequently

for example

however

afterward

1 I have experience flipping pizza dough; _____, I have eaten just about every kind of pizza you can imagine!

2 They will attend the graduation ceremony from 4:00–6:00 p.m., and _____ they will enjoy the banquet.

3 Cinderella had to learn how to get along with her sisters; _____, I am trying to learn ways to get along with my brothers.

4 The concert promoters worked very hard; _____, they did not manage to raise enough money to cover their expenses.

5 The pilot ignored his own good judgement, and _____, the passengers endured a rough landing.

6 Southwest Middle School offers many programs; _____, we have a special club just for whale watching fans.

7 I was disappointed by the movie; _____, I have to agree that it was a technically amazing production.

8 Fast-food chains are producing high-fat combination meals; _____, the American population faces a growing epidemic of obesity.

Traits of Good Writing • 6–8 © 2004 Creative Teaching Press

Stop Those Run-Ons

RUN-ON SENTENCES

Sometimes we overuse a conjunction and thereby create a run-on sentence.
Run-on: We went to the store and we bought what we needed for dinner and then we
   cooked our meal.
Rewrite: We went to the store and bought what we needed for dinner. Then we cooked our meal.

Read each run-on sentence. Rewrite it into a passage that contains fluent sentences.

1 I wanted an ice-cream cone **but** the truck was too fast **and** I tried to run after it **but** there was too much noise for the driver to hear me.

_____

_____

_____

2 I could wear pants today **or** I could wear shorts **but** it might get too cold by lunch **and** since I need to walk to my afternoon piano lesson I think I would be too uncomfortable **and** if I'm uncomfortable then I won't be able to play well.

_____

_____

_____

3 I really wanted a chance to score the winning run **but** I knew that my chances were slim **and** my teammates would understand if I struck out **but** even though I was under a lot of pressure **and** I was very nervous I still managed to get on base.

_____

_____

_____

4 My family went to the beach on Saturday **and** we planned to swim all day **but** when we arrived it began to rain **and** because we didn't have anything else to do we decided to stay and play.

_____

_____

_____

Traits of Good Writing • 6–8 © 2004 Creative Teaching Press

Name _____ Date _____

Fluency Fix

ADDING PUNCTUATION

Add punctuation to the paragraph below to clarify the writer's thoughts and make them more fluent.

You must be kidding how can I possibly finish all this homework and still find time to clean up this mess I never imagined that one puppy could create so many messes in just a few hours didn't I lock the gate before I went to school yesterday my mom clearly reminded me never to leave the puppy out alone now I see what she means she will be home soon if I don't get this house back in order by then the puppy and I will both be looking for a new home.

_____
_____
_____
_____
_____
_____
_____
_____
_____
_____
_____
_____
_____
_____
_____

Traits of Good Writing • 6–8 © 2004 Creative Teaching Press

Too Many Words

REDUCING WORDINESS

Wordiness can sometimes inhibit fluency. Eliminating words to keep your message clear and simple can be a good strategy to improve your writing skills.
> **Example:** The bakery has plenty of doughnuts to sell to its customers.
> **Revision:** The bakery has plenty of doughnuts to sell.

You can eliminate "to its customers" because anyone who buys a doughnut is obviously a customer. There is no one else to whom the bakery will be selling.

Read each sentence. Cross out the words you think are redundant or unnecessary. Rewrite each sentence.

1 The librarian put the books away on the shelf in the library.

Revision: _____

2 I went ice skating on the ice at the ice skating rink.

Revision: _____

3 The female girl was unable to descend down the stairs by herself.

Revision: _____

4 We need the help of a few volunteers to assist us.

Revision: _____

5 Jacob was hired and now is employed by the local grocery food store.

Revision: _____

6 Erica is a smart and intelligent girl.

Revision: _____

7 My sister usually tries to combine together too many colors.

Revision: _____

8 We decided that now, at this point in time, we would not stop for dinner.

Revision: _____

Traits of Good Writing • 6–8 © 2004 Creative Teaching Press

Too Much Business

WRITING CONCISELY

A business letter requires a special kind of fluency. The writing needs to be concise and clear. It should not contain flowery language.

Read this business letter. Rewrite it to reflect correct business form.

❖ **IMO** ❖

Dearest Ms. Richards:

It is with deepest concern that I write this letter informing you of the unknown location of my recent order. I purchased a beautiful green sweater from your fine establishment. The order was quite easily placed on your extensive and enjoyable web site. I plan to gift my grandmother with this most elegant piece of clothing.

I received, quite promptly I would add, a confirmation of my order and the following code of receipt: ES011224B. Unfortunately, much to my dismay, I never received a notification that this lovely garment was placed on a mode of transportation to eventually find its way to my dwelling.

I would be forever indebted to you if you could find it in your heart to assist me in this most concerning affair. I can be reached via phone, fax, letter, e-mail, telegram, voice mail, or any other method of communication available to you. I will wait with baited breath for your reply.

Most Sincerely Yours,
I.M. Overwriter

_____
_____
_____
_____
_____
_____
_____
_____
_____
_____

Traits of Good Writing • 6–8 © 2004 Creative Teaching Press

Name _____ Date _____

Poetic Fluency

RHYTHM AND RHYME

Using rhyming words is one way to add rhythm and fluency to poetry. When writing, brainstorm many different rhyming words for each word you use. This will enable you to have more interesting vocabulary to choose from and provide you with many ideas for the direction of your poem.

Brainstorm a list of rhyming words for each word.

day
_____
_____
_____
_____

there
_____
_____
_____
_____

one
_____
_____
_____
_____

friend
_____
_____
_____
_____

be
_____
_____
_____
_____

fire
_____
_____
_____
_____

street
_____
_____
_____
_____

beach
_____
_____
_____
_____

new
_____
_____
_____
_____

dog
_____
_____
_____
_____

cat
_____
_____
_____
_____

car
_____
_____
_____
_____

Use two sets of rhyming words from your list to write a poem.

_____
_____
_____
_____
_____
_____
_____
_____
_____
_____

Traits of Good Writing • 6–8 © 2004 Creative Teaching Press

Name _____ Date _____

Conversation with Yourself

FREE EXPRESSION

> Journal writing is one way to express your thoughts and feelings effortlessly. Sentence fluency comes naturally in free writing, much as it does in natural speech.

Write a short journal entry about each topic. Then reread your entry and pay attention to the ease with which your sentences flow.

1 Your most embarrassing moment

_____
_____
_____
_____
_____
_____

2 The best thing that ever happened to you

_____
_____
_____
_____
_____
_____

3 A time you will never forget

_____
_____
_____
_____
_____
_____

4 The funniest thing you ever saw or did

_____
_____
_____
_____
_____

Traits of Good Writing • 6–8 © 2004 Creative Teaching Press

Prepare for Necessity

SPELLING

Circle the spelling errors in this fable. Write each misspelled word below and then write the correct spelling beside it.

The Ant and the Grasshopper
Aesop's Fable

In a feild one summer's day a grasshopper was hoping about, chirping and singing to its heart's content. An ant past by, bearing along with grate toil an ear of corn he was taking to the nest.

"Why not come and chat with me," asked the grasshopper, "instead of toiling and moiling in that way?"

"I am helping to lay up food for the winter," said the ant, "and reccomend you to do the same."

"Why bother about winter?" said the grasshopper. "We've got plenty of food at present."

But the ant went on it's way and continued its toil. When the winter come, the grasshopper had no food and found itself dieing of hunger, while it saw the ants every day distributing corn and grain from the stores they had collected in the summer. Then the grasshopper new:

It is best to prepare for the days of neccesity.

Misspelled Word	**Correct Spelling**
❶ _____	_____
❷ _____	_____
❸ _____	_____
❹ _____	_____
❺ _____	_____
❻ _____	_____
❼ _____	_____
❽ _____	_____
❾ _____	_____
❿ _____	_____

Circle the word in each pair that is spelled correctly.

⓫ absence   abcense   ⓭ maintanence   maintenance

⓬ calendar   calender   ⓮ potatos   potatoes

Name _____ Date _____

Homophone Help

SPELLING

Circle the correct homophone to complete each sentence.

1 You are not (allowed, aloud) to use a calculator on this test.

2 When using a proper noun, remember to use a (capital, capitol) letter.

3 I need a new (pear, pare, pair) of shoes.

4 What will the (weather, whether) be like tomorrow?

5 The doctor was able to see thirty (patience, patients) a day.

6 Don't stand (by, bye, buy) that dog; he might be dangerous.

7 If I spend any more money, I won't have enough for cab (fair, fare).

8 Please order me a (plain, plane) hamburger.

9 Joe, did you (write, right) this essay by yourself?

10 You need to (wait, weight) your turn.

11 The (principle, principal) called the students to the gym for an assembly.

12 Gail is a vegetarian, so she does not eat (meat, meet).

13 Goodbye, Mom! I'll be home in an (our, hour).

14 Will you go to the store with me? The shirt I want to buy is on (sale, sail).

15 Is that bench made of (wood, would)?

Traits of Good Writing • 6–8 © 2004 Creative Teaching Press

Name _____ Date _____

Trip to Bayfield

APPOSITIVES

An **appositive** is a word or phrase that gives more information about a previous noun or pronoun.
Our teacher, Miss Pickrell, loves grammar.
"Miss Pickrell" is in apposition to "Our teacher" and explains who our teacher is.

Use the appositives from the word box to fill in the blanks.

Jenny May	our uncle's estate	Ian and Betsy
those black carry-ons	daffodils, crocuses, and tulips	their uncle

1 Would you please help us reach our bags, _____, on the top shelf?

2 We are headed to Bayfield, _____ , to spend the last of our winter holidays.

3 The snow is melting and the Drew cousins, _____, are busy helping Jerry, _____, in the garden while their aunt, _____, is baking fresh, blueberry pies indoors.

4 They are planting a variety of spring flowers, _____, under the bay trees.

5 Place an X by the phrases that could be used as appositives.
_____ a rye bread sandwich
_____ after they ate
_____ slowly and carefully
_____ a Southern state

Use your own appositives to complete each sentence.

6 Their children, _____, are away at present, visiting their friend, _____ , in Japan.

7 As they walked in the door, they could smell their aunt's special dessert, _____ .

8 Uncle Jerry inherited the estate, _____, from George and Kate, _____ .

Traits of Good Writing • 6–8 © 2004 Creative Teaching Press

Name _____ Date _____

Dear Sir

PUNCTUATION

> **Semicolons** help separate sentences when a conjunction, such as *but, and,* or *or,* is not used.
> **Colons** come before lists, after a greeting in a business letter, and in numbers to tell time.

Insert the correct punctuation (semicolons, colons, commas, or periods) in each sentence.

1 This is such an odd combination of words __ stones__wine__chimney__quotient__ __Apsen__cat___ and Puffy___

2 An appositive is a phrase that modifies a noun____clauses have verbs and subjects___.

Rewrite each letter. Add the correct punctuation.

1 Dear Manager
I am writing to inform you about some problems with your products and shipping I ordered the following computer equipment from your website a modem a mouse a keyboard and a hard drive They arrived scratched and dented

_____
_____
_____
_____
_____

2 Dear April
It was so lovely to have tea with you last week I know you heard about my poor foot I have to tell you about the accident It was so careless of me I would love to have you stay for a while to help me around the house
Please come as soon as you can It will be so fun to see you Jim Missy and Mary are excited to see you too

_____
_____
_____
_____
_____

Traits of Good Writing • 6–8 © 2004 Creative Teaching Press

Name _____ Date _____

Local News

> A **direct quotation** gives the exact words someone wrote or said. An **indirect quotation** restates or rephrases something that was said or written. Quotation marks are not used.

Indirect quote: The headlines today said that a malfunction caused a train wreck.
Direct quote: The headlines today read, "Malfunction Caused Train Wreck."

Change these indirect quotes into direct quotes with the correct punctuation.

1 The Daily Paper reported the price of milk was going up from $2.00 to $2.50 per gallon.

_____

2 The City section reported that crime was on the rise in the metropolitan area.

_____

3 Detective Jones said that three bicycles were stolen from the Main Street Park in the last month.

_____

4 Denise Porter, an F.B.I agent, added the statement that extra police officers would be assigned to areas of high traffic.

_____

5 Imagine you are a reporter covering the local news. Write a short informative article using direct quotations.

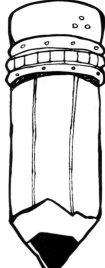

_____
_____
_____
_____
_____
_____
_____
_____
_____
_____
_____

Traits of Good Writing • 6–8 © 2004 Creative Teaching Press

Bus Delays

PUNCTUATION

> **Quotation marks** are used for direct quotes and dialog. A direct quotation gives the exact words someone wrote or said.

Indicate if the statements are correctly punctuated. Write **C** for correct and **I** for incorrect.

_____ **1** "Watch out! they cried."

_____ **2** "Quick, Benny! The bus is coming!" Jill shouted.

_____ **3** They informed the school principal that, "The bus was late."

_____ **4** Teachers heard the announcement. Good morning students and teachers. One of our buses is running late.

_____ **5** The bus driver said calmly, students please be seated. We are running a bit late due to the weather.

_____ **6** Oh no. We will miss our math test, Jill, Do you think they will wait for us? asked Benny.

_____ **7** As the bus pulled into the parking lot, Benny said he was sure their teacher would wait for their arrival.

Rewrite the incorrect sentences above using the correct punctuation marks.

8 _____

9 _____

10 _____

11 _____

12 _____

Traits of Good Writing • 6–8 © 2004 Creative Teaching Press

Two or More

NOUNS

The plural form of most nouns is created simply by adding the letter *s,* such as changing *snake* to *snakes.* Some nouns have irregular plural forms, such as changing *child* to *children.*

Change each singular noun to its plural form.

	Singular	**Plural**		**Singular**	**Plural**
1	leaf	_____	10	cargo	_____
2	account	_____	11	mouse	_____
3	monkey	_____	12	giraffe	_____
4	anxiety	_____	13	medium	_____
5	suburb	_____	14	formula	_____
6	champagne	_____	15	ox	_____
7	laugh	_____	16	homework	_____
8	radius	_____	17	excess	_____
9	misunderstanding	_____	18	property	_____

Change each plural noun to its singular form.

	Plural	**Singular**		**Plural**	**Singular**
19	teeth	_____	25	foxes	_____
20	moose	_____	26	cries	_____
21	calves	_____	27	decks	_____
22	dreams	_____	28	elves	_____
23	mosquitoes	_____	29	women	_____
24	potatoes	_____	30	crimes	_____

Traits of Good Writing • 6–8 © 2004 Creative Teaching Press

Common vs. Proper Nouns

NOUNS

Common nouns name a person, place, or thing. **Proper nouns** name a specific person, place, or thing. All proper nouns begin with a capital letter.

Rewrite the nouns. Make sure to capitalize all proper nouns.

1 road _____
main street _____
driveway _____

2 africa _____
continent _____
europe _____

3 river _____
stream _____
amazon _____

4 day _____
Thursday _____
Afternoon _____

5 mt. Rushmore _____
statue _____
mountain _____

person place thing

Write two proper nouns for each common noun.

6 author _____   _____

7 building _____   _____

8 bridge _____   _____

9 city _____   _____

10 state _____   _____

11 holiday _____   _____

12 artist _____   _____

13 ocean _____   _____

14 magazine _____   _____

15 month _____   _____

Traits of Good Writing • 6–8 © 2004 Creative Teaching Press

Name _____ Date _____

Possessive Nouns

NOUNS

> An apostrophe and an *s* can be added to singular and plural nouns to show possession.

Singular possessive nouns: add an apostrophe and an *s*   boy's hand
Plural possessive noun not ending in *s*: add an apostrophe and an *s*   children's voices
Plural possessive ending with *s*:   add an apostrophe after the *s* teachers' papers

Correct each sentence by writing the possessive form of the underlined word on the line.

1 The <u>child</u> shoes were dirty. _____

2 The teacher had all of her <u>student</u> attention. _____

3 The <u>doctor</u> office is busy. _____

4 The <u>principal</u> tie is very colorful. _____

5 The <u>children</u> work was displayed on the walls. _____

6 The <u>boy</u> drawings were very detailed. _____

7 <u>Mrs. Kelly</u> stories are the best! _____

8 The <u>men</u> basketball team is undefeated. _____

9 The <u>mothers</u> club holds a bake sale every year. _____

10 Please respect other <u>people</u> property. _____

11 The <u>kitten</u> toys are missing. _____

12 The <u>women</u> race was about to begin. _____

13 Write a paragraph about something that happened in one of your classes. Use at least three different possessive nouns.

_____
_____
_____
_____
_____
_____
_____

Traits of Good Writing • 6-8 © 2004 Creative Teaching Press

Name _____ Date _____

Homecoming

PRONOUNS

> A **pronoun** is a word that takes the place of a noun. Pronouns like *we, our, they, I, he, it,* and *she* may be the subjects of a sentence. Pronouns like *him, her, them, us, me, you,* and *it* can be used as direct objects in a sentence.

Read each sentence. Write **C** if the underlined pronoun is used correctly. Write **I** if it is used incorrectly.

_____ **1** The sports club committee invited <u>his</u> to their anniversary dinner.

_____ **2** My parents and <u>me</u> have been invited to the wedding reception.

_____ **3** Charlie gave his old bike to <u>his</u> younger brother, Tim.

_____ **4** As part of the study program, the American students traveled as a team to <u>they</u> destination in Hamburg, Germany.

_____ **5** <u>Our</u> class trip to the Zoological Gardens was the best of the school year.

_____ **6** I am waiting for directions to the party for Andrew and <u>me.</u>

_____ **7** Do you know how <u>us</u> should proceed?

_____ **8** The building permit did not allow <u>him</u> to remove the old fence.

Complete the sentences with pronouns from the word box. Some words may be used more than once.

our	their	her	its	it	he	them	my	his

Our high school has just finished building (9)_____ own football field. We are holding (10)_____ first homecoming football game there next month. The alumni have been invited and 75% of (11)_____ are expected to turn out for the special events planned. I am looking forward to (12)_____. (13)_____ friend, Mandy, is a cheerleader. (14)_____ grandparents are coming from Florida especially to see her and (15)_____ brother this year. Jimmy, her brother, is playing quarterback, and (16)_____ is looking forward to (17)_____ first homecoming game this year also. Mandy says that (18)_____ grandparents are sweet, and that they like to talk about (19)_____ talented grandchildren to (20)_____ neighbors back home.

Traits of Good Writing • 6–8 © 2004 Creative Teaching Press

Action Verbs

VERBS

An **action verb** expresses action in a sentence. It tells what the subject of the sentence does.

Underline the action verbs.

1 George bought a new bike.

2 He looked at many different bikes in order to find the right one.

3 George raced his new bike down the hill.

4 He didn't see the large pothole in the street.

5 The bike's front tire exploded.

6 George walked his bike to the shop.

7 He knew the people at the bike shop would be surprised to see him again.

8 The shop owner, Mr. Hamilton, laughed as George entered.

9 Then he realized that George needed help.

10 Mr. Hamilton fixed George's bike.

11 Write a short paragraph telling what George does next. Underline all the action verbs you use.

_____

_____

_____

_____

_____

_____

_____

_____

_____

_____

_____

Traits of Good Writing • 6–8 © 2004 Creative Teaching Press

Name _____ Date _____

Lend Me a Helping Verb!

VERBS

At times, the main verb, or action, in a sentence is supported by another verb called a **helping verb.** A helping verb helps the main verb show action. It cannot stand by itself.

Choose an appropriate helping verb from the word box to complete each sentence.

is	was	has	could	were	can
are	will	have	am	had	

1 We _____ drive to the beach.

2 Tommy _____ writing a story.

3 Gail _____ performed many times before.

4 She _____ trying her hardest to perform well.

5 Sandra and I _____ help her get it right.

6 They _____ running as fast as they could.

7 Tony _____ played trumpet for three years.

8 Everybody _____ packing the car for the trip.

9 My friends _____ joined the band.

10 Debbie and I _____ practicing our spelling words.

11 Our teacher _____ reading the story.

12 The doctor _____ checking the patient.

13 The coaches _____ discussing their strategy.

14 The team _____win the game.

15 We _____ made many mistakes.

Traits of Good Writing • 6–8 © 2004 Creative Teaching Press

Name _____ Date _____

Play Ball!

DIRECT/INDIRECT OBJECTS

A **direct object** follows a verb and completes its meaning.
I ate an <u>apple</u>.
Indirect objects are words that come between the verb and direct object. These words usually tell whom or for whom something is done.
I gave <u>him</u> a card.

Identify the verb and direct/indirect objects in each sentence.

1 The proud coach handed Randy and his teammates the beautiful trophy.
Verb(s) _____
Direct Object(s) _____
Indirect Object(s) _____

2 The Bulldog coach did not give Harry any criticisms after the game.
Verb(s) _____
Direct Object(s) _____
Indirect Object(s) _____

3 Robert and Kate gave Randy a huge hug that night and promised their nephew a reward for his victory.
Verb(s) _____
Direct Object(s) _____
Indirect Object(s) _____

4 Underline the direct objects. Circle the indirect objects.

Randy's team, the Bulldogs, are having a good season this year. They celebrated a victory over the Cardinals. Coach Danny congratulated the team and gave Randy an encouraging pat on the back for a job well done.

Yesterday, Randy and his baseball friends played and won the most exciting game so far. The team had the bases loaded in the ninth inning. Then the Cardinal pitcher, Harry, threw Randy a fast curve ball. Randy hit a home run and the team won the game. The crowd gave Randy and the team a standing ovation. The Bulldogs played an exciting game!

Traits of Good Writing • 6–8 © 2004 Creative Teaching Press

Who?

TRANSITIVE VERBS

A **transitive verb** is a verb that has a direct object.
> Mike carried <u>the ball</u>.

An **intransitive verb** is a verb that does not have a direct object.
> We arrived late.

After reading a sentence, say the verb and ask *what* or *whom*. If the sentence answers the question, the verb is transitive.

Most verbs can be used either way.
> Eliza <u>met</u> the director.
> Eliza and the director <u>met</u> later.

Underline the verb in each sentence. Write a **T** before the sentence if the verb is transitive. Write an **I** if it is intransitive.

1 _____ Sarah laughed so hard that she cried.

2 _____ We drove to the track meet.

3 _____ The children recycled the cans from their lunches.

4 _____ The rain caused a great flood across the country.

5 _____ The map gave detailed clues to the mystery.

6 _____ The dog dug frantically to hide his bone.

7 _____ The scientists explored the cave for animal bones.

8 _____ The choir sang beautifully at the concert.

9 _____ We painted the mural on the wall near the playground.

10 _____ It had a coating of paint all over it.

11 _____ The family chose their vacation destination carefully.

12 _____ Swimmers would dive into the cold water.

13 _____ The children peeked out from under the pile of leaves.

14 _____ I accept the award on behalf of the whole school.

15 _____ Mary borrowed my pencil for the test.

Traits of Good Writing • 6–8 © 2004 Creative Teaching Press

Principle Parts of Verbs

VERB TENSE

The four basic ways a verb can be changed to show the time of an action are called the **principle parts.**

Present	Present Participle	Past	Past Participle
try	(is) trying	tried	(has) tried
walk	(is) walking	walked	(has) walked

Use a form of *be* with the present participle – I <u>am trying</u> to remember.
Use a form of *have* with the past participle – I <u>have tried</u> before.

Underline the verb or verb phrase in each sentence. Then name its principle part.

1 _____ Caroline is making a present for her grandmother.

2 _____ Mr. Ryan has taught history for twelve years.

3 _____ We brought a new scoreboard for the gym.

4 _____ Please place your paper on the pile when you finish.

5 _____ The keys are lying on the table in the hall.

Change each verb or verb phrase as indicated in parentheses.

6 use (past participle) _____   **7** join (past) _____

8 design (present participle) _____   **9** muttered (present) _____

10 is assembling (past participle) _____

Complete this chart showing principle parts.

Present	Present Participle	Past	Past Participle
11 work	_____	_____	_____
12 _____	is noticing	_____	_____
13 _____	is drying	dried	_____
14 gasp	_____	_____	has gasped

Traits of Good Writing • 6–8 © 2004 Creative Teaching Press

Name _____ Date _____

Irregular Verbs

VERBS

> **Irregular verbs** do not form the past and past participle by adding *-d* or *-ed*. These verbs are best learned by memorizing.

Verb	Past	Past Participle
catch	caught	(has) caught
give	gave	(has) given
know	knew	(has) known
eat	ate	(has) eaten
swim	swam	(has) swum
think	thought	(has) thought
go	went	(has) gone

Change the verb in parentheses to the correct past or past participle form.

1 The center fielder _____ the ball. (catch)

2 We _____ the answers to all the questions on the test. (know)

3 Mary has _____ in her grandmother's pond every summer. (swim)

4 Did you know we had _____ that shirt as a gift? (give)

5 I _____ you would want to travel in an airplane. (think)

6 We should have _____ earlier to avoid the traffic. (go)

7 My teacher _____ me advice on my science fair project. (give)

8 The child had _____ her cold while at school. (catch)

9 We _____ in our new bathing suits yesterday. (swim)

10 I should have _____ breakfast before leaving for school. (eat)

11 My father _____ to school in Minnesota. (go)

12 He should have _____ the way to the museum. (know)

13 The class _____ lunch on the playground under the tree. (eat)

14 She has _____ about her present all week. (think)

15 Have you _____ on vacation every year? (go)

Traits of Good Writing • 6–8 © 2004 Creative Teaching Press

Name _____ Date _____

Vacation Time

Grammar

Spelling, punctuation, grammar, and capitalization are all important writing conventions that help make your writing more readable. Without them, a reader would have a difficult time hearing your message because the text would be confusing and hard to read.

Copy Editor's Symbols

℮ Take it out

∧ Put something in

⊙ Add a period

m̲ Make this a capital letter

M̸ Make this a lowercase letter

(error) Spelling error

∧# Put in a space

Use the copy editor's symbols to correct the errors in this passage.

Summer is the caribbean's off-season, which means you'll get low rates, beautiful beaches; mild breezes, and a quiet beachfront hammock all to yourself. You might like tobook a flight to Montego bay or Jamaica. If you like crystal-clear waters, windsurfing, and snorkleing, Grand Bahama Island is the place for you.

Swimming not your strength? Then head farther south to visit argentina or Chile. The seasons here are reversed, and you can go skiing in July. Buenos Aires is a great place to do a little shopping during your visit.

Whatever you choose, youd be smart to book your flight now. Summeris almost hear and you are not the only kid on the block who'll be heading south.

Traits of Good Writing • 6–8 © 2004 Creative Teaching Press

Error Hunt

Grammar

> Spelling, punctuation, grammar, and capitalization are all important writing conventions that help make your writing more readable. Without them, a reader would have a difficult time hearing your message because the text would be confusing and hard to read.

Copy Editor's Symbols

_e_ Take it out

∧ Put something in

⊙ Add a period

_m_ Make this a capital letter

M Make this a lowercase letter

(error) Spelling error

∧# Put in a space

Use the copy editor's symbols to correct the errors in this passage.

Do you no what happens every time you take a step, cross your legs, or stoop to tie your shoe? Your knees are working hard. knees are among the most vulnarable joints in the body. They take a greatdeal of stress every day, and they absorb much of the impact from runing or jogging. To increese your knee strength, boost the surrounding mussles, which act as a support system. You can Strengthen these muscles by doing exercises, such as knee extensions, wall squats, and hamstring curls. Maintaning a a healthy weight an wearing the a proper footwear while walkingjogging will also help you maintain healthy knee jonts. the next time you you step onto that skateboard or run down a basketball court, remember how hard your knees are working for you. Take good care of them!

Traits of Good Writing • 6-8 © 2004 Creative Teaching Press

Answer Key

Writer's Notebook (page 5)

Answers will vary.

Take Another Look (page 6)

Answer will vary.

Name That Genre (page 7)

1. fantasy
2. science fiction
3. romance
4. mystery
5. historical fiction
6. comedy
7. science fiction

Sentence Stretch (page 8)

Answers will vary.

Like a Person (page 9)

Answers will vary.

Hold Up (page 10)

1. post office, windows, mailbox, mailbag, blinds, customers
2. It appeared to be an ordinary day at the post office.
A. flag waved brightly in the breeze
B. closed windows glistened in the morning light
C. mailbox stood proudly to the right of the main entrance
3. But something was wrong, Jarrod observed.
A. mailbag sat on the ground unattended
B. blinds were shut
C. customers had entered the post office but no one had left
4. Answers will vary.

Crazy Characters (page 11)

Physical Characteristics:
Haphazard ponytail
Backwards cap
Wears big, baggy clothes
Personality Traits:
Very care-free
Acts like a tomboy
Loves skateboarding

Habits:
Skateboards everyday after school
Blows bubbles constantly
Is at home alone part of each day
Answers will vary.

Invention Convention (page 12)

1. Problem: Many people have problems biting their finger-nails.
A. Require them to paint their fingernails with a nasty-tasting polish.
B. Require them to wear acrylic nails that are too thick to bite or tear.
C. Invent the "anti-nail-biting machine."
2–4. Answers will vary.

Cause and Effect (page 13)

1. <u>Cause:</u> The California Gold Rush
<u>Effect:</u> People traveled from the east coast by land or around South America by boat.
<u>Cause:</u> Growing population and presence of more currency
<u>Effect:</u> Prices of food, clothing, and tools were driven up.
<u>Cause:</u> Merchants made haste to take advantage of business opportunities.
<u>Effect:</u> Businesses sprang up everywhere.
<u>Cause:</u> Gold Rush
<u>Effect:</u> Some found fortunes and others lost fortunes.
2. Answers will vary.

Food Fair (page 14)

1. <u>Cause:</u> scrumptious, mouthwatering
<u>Effect:</u> satisfies your sweet tooth
<u>Cause:</u> Filled with nuts, chocolate chips, and sunflower seeds
<u>Effect:</u> Provides all-day energy
2. scrumptious, mouth-watering satisfaction
crunchy cookies
all-day energy
tall glass of milk

affordable family staple
homemade quality
3. Buy two boxes for the price of one.
4. while supplies last
5. Answers will vary.

Break It Down (page 15)

1. B
2. E
3. A
4. D
5. C
6–9. Answers will vary.

Biography Blizzard (page 16)

Answers will vary.

Topic Turmoil (page 17)

Answers will vary.

Experiencing Details (page 18)

1. M
2. R
3. M
4. S
5. S
6. R
7. R
8. M
9. S
10. S
11. M
12. R
13. S
14. M
15. R
16. M
17. S
18. S
19. R
20. R

Give Texture to Your Writing (page 19)

Rosebushes can be one of the most rewarding flowers to grow.

Supporting details: 1, 4, 6, 7

Playing professional roller hockey has been Lori's lifelong dream.

Supporting details: 2, 3, 4, 5, 7

Which One Doesn't Belong? (page 20)

1. Red and yellow are primary colors.
2. Sporting equipment is expensive.
3. Handwritten notes are more personal.
4. Gas prices may vary by region.
5. I learned to ride my bicycle when I was in first grade.
6. Mike is allergic to cats.

Unpack Your Ideas (page 21)

1. Bridal Veil Falls
2. Half Dome
3. El Capitan
4. Yosemite Falls
5. Yosemite Valley
6. magnificent, granite
7. cascading
8. thunderous
9. dominates the skyline
10. a giant sentinel
11. Answers will vary.

Picture Perfect! (page 22)

Answers will vary.

In a Nutshell (page 23)

Answers will vary.

Writer's Lingo (page 24)

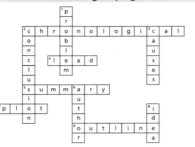

Grab the Reader's Interest (page 25)

Answers will vary.

In the News (page 26)

1. S
2. W
3. W
4. S
5. W

Answers will vary.

Get the Point! (page 27)

1. Many students struggle to keep up with their homework. Learning to (A) set priorities, (B) avoid distractions, and (C) create a reward system will help students improve their homework management skills.
2. Kindness is an important and valuable trait. You can demonstrate kindness (A) by asking people how they are doing, (B) listening to what they tell you, and (C) thinking of creative ways to help others.
3. Recycling is good for the Earth. Creating a recycling program requires (A) carefully analyzing the community's needs, (B) sharing information with all community members, and (C) providing support for people as they begin to recycle in their homes and businesses.

Wide Angle and Close-Up (page 28)

Wide Angle	Close-Up
A	B
D	C
E	G
F	H

Magnetic Writing (page 29)

Answers will vary.

Hobby City (page 30)

The Writer
4, 1, 6, 2, 3, 5
The Gardener
7, 5, 1, 2, 4, 6, 3
The Remote Control Pilot
8, 1, 5, 2, 3, 4, 7, 6

Life Events (page 31)

Answers will vary.

Calculated Conclusions (page 32)

Answers will vary.

Weighty Arguments (page 33)

1. Exercise strengthens your muscles and bones.
Exercise improves your blood circulation.
Exercise is a great way to relieve stress.
2. 3,1,2
3–4. Answers will vary.

Vote for Me (page 34)

1. Draw a line through:
most popular girls in class are my friends
our principal likes me the best of all the candidates
2. 3, 1, 2
3. Vote for me because I'm involved with many school activities, I am generally a good student and maintain good grades, and I will listen to your concerns.

Category Sort (page 35)

1. B
2. C
3. A
4. B
5. A
6. C
7. C
8. A
9. B
Answers will vary.

Managing Internet Searches (page 36)

1. B
2. B
3. A
4. B
5. A, D
6. E
7. B
8. C
9. E
10. D, E

Get Your Facts Straight (page 37)

I. Geography B, D, L
II. History E, G, N
III. Government A, H, M
IV. Cultural Arts F, K
V. Food C, I, J

Transition Chart (page 38)

Location
amid
in back of
beneath
above
Compare and Contrast
similarly
otherwise
even so
in the same way
however
Time
in the meantime
first
after a while

Conclude or Summarize
finally
in conclusion
as a result
to sum up

Find That Transition (page 39)

The following words and phrases should be underlined:
before, next, even so, when, first, on the other hand, otherwise, once, however
Sentences will vary.

In Other Words (page 40)

Answers will vary.

It's a Wrap (page 41)

Answers will vary.

Rocket Writing (page 42)

1. introduction
2. thesis statement
3. point one
4. point two
5. point three
6. restatement of thesis
7. conclusion

Bon Appétit! (page 43)

1–4. 1, 2
5–8. Answers will vary.

Wok Express (page 44)

1–4. 2, 3
5–8. Answers will vary.

Dear Madam (page 45)

Answers will vary.

Out of Town (page 46)

1. second
2. third
3. second
4. third
5. first
6–9. Answers will vary.

Rumors (page 47)

1. C
2. I
3. C
4. I
5. C
6. I
7. I
8. C
9–11. Answers will vary.

Mr. Wolf (page 48)

Answers will vary.

What They Saw (page 49)

Answers will vary.

Ever After (page 50)

Answers will vary.

Grocery List (page 51)

Answers will vary.

E-Voice (page 52)

Answers will vary.

Describe That Voice (page 53)

Answers will vary.

If Voice Were… (page 54)

Answers will vary.

Greeting Card Sentiments (page 55)

Answers will vary.

Using Your Voice (page 56)

Answers will vary.

Different Voices (page 57)

1. excited
2. factual
3. skeptical
4. scientific
5–8. Answers will vary.

Whose Voice Is That? (page 58)

Answers will vary.

Sleep and Dream (page 59)

Answers will vary.

Spiders and Things (page 60)

Answers will vary.

Contrasts (page 61)

Answers will vary.

Familiar or Foreign? (page 62)

1. b
2. c
3. b
4. a
5. a
6. c
7. b
8. a

Heads and Tails (page 63)

1. D mono-
2. F bi-
3. H sub-
4. B super-
5. E inter-
6. G intra-
7. C circum-
8. A trans-
9–14. Answers will vary.

Suffix Sense (page 64)

1. G -ful
2. A -ist
3. D -ly
4. F -ment
5. B -ward
6. H -ible
7. C -less
8. E -or
9–12. Answers will vary.

Verb Makeover (65)

Answers will vary. Possible answers include:
1. moved: rolled, chugged, climbed
2. burned: crackled, blackened, scorched
3. spilled: poured, spewed, shot
4. slid: coasted, slipped, glided
5. blew: whisked, wafted, fanned

Answers will vary. Possible answers include:
<u>said</u>
announced
related
expressed
asserted
responded
<u>walked</u>
trampled
strolled
roamed
ambled
trudged
<u>cried</u>
wept
sobbed
wailed
mourned
whimpered
<u>slept</u>
dozed
napped
snoozed
hibernated
catnapped

Don't Just Sit There! (page 66)

1. P
2. A
3. P
4. P
5. A
6. A
7. P
8. P
9. A
10. A
11. Most of the class is reading the book.
12. She slammed on the brakes when she saw the red light.
13. The PTA committee is considering the proposal.
14. The school board approved the new policy.
15. The judge gave the novice musician an excellent score.

First Day (page 67)

1. cleaner, cleanest
2. more colorful, most colorful
3. stronger, strongest
4. greener, greenest
5. more disruptive, most disruptive
6. more secure, most secure
7. healthier, healthiest
8. lovelier, loveliest
9. more terrifying, most terrifying
10. more talkative, most talkative

Answers will vary. Possible answers include:
11. secure
12. cleanest
13. greener, lovely
14. more colorful
15. stronger

Adding Details (page 68)

1. verb: lives
adverb: upstairs (where)
2. verb: calls
adverb: often (how often)
3. verb: ran
adverb: swiftly (how)
4. verb: moved
adverb: slowly (how)
5. verb: leave
adverb: here (where)
6. verb: pecking
adverb: eagerly (how)
7. verb: return
adverb: before (when)
8. verb: made
adverb: quickly (how)
9. verb: finished
adverb: first (when)
10. verb: takes
adverb: every day (how often)
11. verb: soared
adverb: above (where)
12. verb: works
adverb: enthusiastically (how)
13. verb: barked
adverb: fiercely (how)
14. verb: waiting
adverb: patiently (how)

15. verb: naps
adverb: frequently (how often)
16. verb: listen
adverb: carefully (how)

Storm Warning (page 69)

1. clearer, clearest
2. transparent, most transparent
3. quicker, quickest
4. more decisive, most decisive
5. farther, farthest
6. Suddenly, hysterically, merrily
7. Immediately, firmly, speedily
8. nearby, quickly, breathlessly, vaguely, briefly
9. more quickly
10. more erratically
11. decisively, urgently, consistently

Moving to the City (page 70)

1. b
2. a
3. b
4. a
5. disastrous
6. annoying, dawn, exhausted
7. refreshing, wearily, anxiously
8. reluctantly

Join 'Em Up (page 71)

1. Even though the rainfall has been light this year, the tropical forest is very damp.
2. Because they narrowly escaped the tiger, the two friends became more cautious.
3. Now that you finished painting the room, the makeover is complete.
4. Justin stood up so that the young child would have a place to sit.
5. Whenever Mrs. Pak bakes cookies, the entire neighborhood stops by for a sample.
6. She decided to go home rather than join her friends at the party.
7. Britney chose to attend college whereas her mother did not have the same opportunity.

Think Again (page 72)

1. defective
2. comprehend
3. tremendous
4. pleasant
5. tolerate
6. conceive
7. receive
8. formidable

Off Limits (page 73)

Answers will vary.

Similar To… (page 74)

1. The following phrases should be underlined:
changeable as the weather
deceptive as a snake
brave as a lion
quick as lightning
silent as the grave
lovely as a rose
bright as day
2–7. Answers will vary.

Create a Mental Picture (page 75)

Answers will vary.

As Big as a Barn (page 76)

Answers will vary.

What Are You Saying? (page 77)

1. G
2. K
3. E
4. J
5. A
6. B
7. M
8. D
9. H
10. C
11. N
12. I
13. L
14. F
15–17. Answers will vary.

Make the Connections (page 78)

1. plane
2. pine
3. waist
4. instrument
5. lungs
6. airplane
7. interruption
8. futuristic
9. literary
10. defeat
11. navigate
12. wrapper
13. dischord

Same Difference (page 79)

1. a unrestricted
2. c inquiring
3. b ambiguous
4. a widespread
5. d convert
6. a mistake
7. b lackluster
8. a fearlessness
9. c conceal
10. a discharged

Think Opposite (page 80)

1. cowardly
2. acknowledge
3. deficient
4. doubt
5. unique
6. artificial
7. surrender
8. conclusion
9. grotesque
10. inattentive
11. mitigate
12. life
13. incompetent
14. brash
15. harmless
16. illegal
17. dislodge
18. irregular
19. unjust
20. joyless
21. inarticulate
22. irresponsible
23. restful
24. indiscreet

25. cheerful
26. disobedient
27. unproductive
28. thoughtless

How Does the Word Make You Feel? (page 81)

1. thinking
2. dancing
3. smiling
4. weeping
5. writing
6. energetic
7. confident
8–9. Answers will vary.

Crickety, Creak (page 82)

1. tick-tock
2. Crickety-creak
3. swishing
4. howl, yelped
5. crackled, hissed
6. creaked, sputter
7. swish
8. splat
9. squeaking
10. boom
11. splash
12. quacking

Sweet Smell of Success (page 83)

The following clichés should be circled:
1. sweet smell of success
a dime a dozen
that's the ticket
jump for joy
lay of the land
as good as gold
bigger and better
2–6. Answers will vary.

Sensory Scene (page 84)

Answers will vary.

Off to a Good Start (page 85)

1–5. Answers will vary.
7. Before his sister could have one bite, Jeremy inhaled the pizza.
8. It began to snow as we made our way to the summit.
9. Before I realized I had dropped my book, my homework assignment fell into the mud.
10. Since it was already Friday, they were surprised to see a good selection of CDs left.

Sentence Sense (page 86)

1–4. Answers will vary.
5. geography
6. stomachs
7. lunch bell
8. friends
9. cafeteria
10. effort
11. lines
12. Jenny
13. table
14. selection

Clause Connection (page 87)

1. D
2. I
3. I
4. D
5. D
6. I
7. I
8. D
9–12. Answers will vary.

Enjoy! (page 88)

Answers will vary. Possible answers include:
1. Bonnie enjoyed drinking tea and eating her noodles while having lunch at the peaceful Chinese Garden restaurant.
2. Everyone who received an invitation attended the spectacular Mayor's Ball.
3. Ellen put on her warm winter coat and furry hat before she left for the concert.
4. The sleepy zookeeper makes his rounds at dawn to be sure that all the animals are fed and the cages are clean.

Sentence Secrets (page 89)

1. sleep (may improve)
2. Hawaii (is known)
3. salt (sprinkled)
4. Spring (brings)
5. Buyers (may upgrade)
6. compound
7. simple
8. complex
9. simple
10. compound

Ball. Ball? Ball! (page 90)

1. interrogative/?
2. exclamatory/!
3. interrogative/?
4. declarative/.
5. exclamatory/!
6. imperative/.
7. imperative/.
8. interrogative/?
9. imperative/.
10. imperative/.
11. exclamatory/!
12. declarative/.
Answers will vary.

Newspaper Search (page 91)

Answers will vary.

Create and Combine (page 92)

Answers will vary. Possible answers include:

1. We ate our picnic lunch at the park one sunny afternoon.
2. Though he was exhausted, his freshly washed car looked shiny and new.
3. Everyone wanted a sample when they smelled Elizabeth's freshly baked cookies.
4. In spite of my initial fears, I am proud of my accomplishment of learning to ski.

Mix It Up (page 93)

Answers will vary. Possible answers include:

1. If your chickens have not yet hatched, don't count them.
2. With all work and no play, our boy Jack is dull.
3. When the cat's away, it is play-time for the mice.
4. The doctor will stay away if each day an apple you eat.
5. Dying with honor is better than the shame with which you live.
6. If you are trying to skin a cat, there are many ways to do it.
7. You should not throw stones, if in a glass house you live.
8. In love and war, all is fair.
9. If you have only one basket, don't put all your eggs in it.
10. The other side of the fence is where the grass is always more green.

Good for Glue (page 94)

Answers will vary.
1. furthermore
2. afterward
3. similarly
4. however
5. consequently
6. for example
7. at the same time
8. meanwhile

Stop Those Run-Ons (page 95)

Answers will vary.

Fluency Fix (page 96)

Answers will vary.

Too Many Words (page 97)

The following words should be crossed out:
1. in the library
2. on the ice, ice
3. female, down
4. to assist us
5. was hired and now, food
6. smart or intelligent
7. together
8. now, at this point in time

Too Much Business (page 98)

Answers will vary.

Poetic Fluency (page 99)

Answers will vary.

Conversation with Yourself (page 100)

Answers will vary.

Prepare for Necessity (page 101)

1. feild, field
2. hoping, hopping
3. past, passed
4. grate, great
5. reccomend, recommend
6. it's, its
7. come, came
8. dieing, dying
9. new, knew
10. neccesity, necessity
11. absence
12. calendar
13. maintenance
14. potatoes

Homophone Help (page 102)

1. allowed
2. capital
3. pair
4. weather
5. patients
6. by
7. fare
8. plain
9. write
10. wait
11. principal
12. meat
13. hour
14. sale
15. wood

Trip to Bayfield (page 103)

1. those black carry-ons
2. our uncle's estate
3. Ian and Betsy; their uncle; Jenny May
4. daffodils, crocuses, and tulips
5. a rye bread sandwich; a Southern state
6–8. Answers will vary.

Dear Sir (page 104)

1. This is such an odd combination of words: stones, wine, chimney, quotient, Aspen, cat, and Puffy.
2. An appositive is a phrase that modifies a noun; clauses have verbs and subjects.

Dear Manager:
  I am writing to inform you about some problems with your products and shipping. I ordered the following computer equipment from your web site: a modem, a mouse, a keyboard, and a hard-drive. They arrived scratched and dented.

Dear April,
  It was so lovely to have tea with you last week. I know you heard about my poor foot. I have to tell you about the accident. It was so careless of me. I would love to have you stay for a while to help me around the house.
  Please come as soon as you can. It will be so fun to see you. Jim, Missy, and Mary are excited to see you, too.

Local News (page 105)

1. The Daily Paper reported, "The price of milk is going up from $2.00 to $2.50 per gallon."
2. The City section reported, "Crime is on the rise in the metropolitan area."
3. Detective Jones said, "Three bicycles were stolen from the Main Street Park in the last month."
4. Denise Porter, an F.B.I. agent stated, "Extra police officers will be assigned to areas of high traffic."
5. Answers will vary.

Bus Delays (page 106)

1. I
2. C
3. I
4. I
5. I
6. I
7. C
8. "Watch out!" they cried.
9. They informed the school principal that the bus was late.
10. Teachers heard the announcement, "Good morning student and teachers. One of our buses is running late."
11. The bus driver said calmly, "Students, please be seated. We are running a bit late due to the weather."
12. "Oh, no! We will miss our math test, Jill. Do you think they will wait for us?" asked Benny.

Two or More (page 107)

1. leaves
2. accounts
3. monkeys
4. anxieties
5. suburbs
6. champagnes
7. laughs
8. radii
9. misunderstandings
10. cargoes
11. mice
12. giraffes
13. mediums or media
14. formulas
15. oxen
16. homework
17. excesses
18. properties
19. tooth
20. moose
21. calf
22. dream
23. mosquito
24. potato
25. fox
26. cry
27. deck
28. elf
29. woman
30. crime

Common vs. Proper Nouns (page 108)

1. road, Main Street, driveway
2. Africa, continent, Europe
3. river, stream, Amazon
4. day, Thursday, afternoon
5. Mt. Rushmore, statue, mountain
6–15. Answers will vary.

Possessive Nouns (page 109)

1. child's
2. students'
3. doctor's
4. principal's
5. children's
6. boy's
7. Mrs. Kelly's
8. men's
9. mothers'
10. people's
11. kitten's
12. women's
13. Answers will vary.

Homecoming (page 110)

1. I
2. I
3. C
4. I
5. C
6. C
7. I
8. C
9. its
10. our
11. them
12. it
13. My
14. Her
15. her
16. he
17. his
18. their
19. their
20. their

Action Verbs (page 111)

1. bought
2. looked
3. raced
4. didn't see
5. exploded
6. walked
7. knew, see
8. laughed
9. realized
10. fixed
11. Answers will vary.

Lend Me a Helping Verb! (page 112)

1. can/will/could
2. is/was
3. has/had
4. is/was
5. will/can/could
6. were
7. has
8. is/was
9. have/had
10. are/were
11. is/was
12. is/was
13. are/were
14. will/can/could
15. have/had

Play Ball! (page 113)

1. verb: handed
direct object: trophy
indirect objects: Randy and
   teammates
2. verb: give
direct object: criticisms
indirect object: Harry
3. verbs: gave; promised
direct objects: hug and reward
indirect objects: Randy and
   nephew
4. The following are direct objects
   and should be underlined:
   season, victory, pat, game, ball,
   home run, standing ovation
The following are indirect objects
and should be circled:
   Randy, the team

Who? (page 114)

1. I, laughed
2. I, drove
3. T, recycled
4. T, caused
5. T, gave
6. I, dug
7. T, explored
8. I, sang
9. T, painted
10. I, had
11. T, chose
12. I, dive
13. I, peeked
14. T, accept
15. T, borrowed

Principle Parts of Verbs (page 115)

1. present participle/is making
2. past participle/has taught
3. past/brought
4. present/place
5. present participle/are lying
6. has used or have used
7. joined
8. is designing or are designing
9. mutter
10. has assembled or have
    assembled
11. is working, worked, has worked
12. notice, noticed, has noticed
13. dry, has dried
14. is gasping, gasped

Irregular Verbs (page 116)

1. caught
2. knew
3. swum
4. given
5. thought
6. gone
7. gave
8. caught
9. swam
10. eaten
11. went
12. known
13. ate
14. thought
15. gone

Summer is the caribbean's off-season, which means you'll get low rates, beautiful beaches, mild breezes, and a quiet beachfront hammock all to yourself. You might like to book a flight to Montego bay or Jamaica. If you like crystal-clear waters, windsurfing, and ~~snorkleing~~ *snorkeling*, Grand Bahama Island is the place for you.

Swimming not your strength? Then head farther south to visit argentina or Chile. The seasons ~~here~~ *there* are reversed, ~~and~~ *so* you can go skiing in July. Buenos Aires is a great place to do a little shopping during your visit.

Whatever you choose, you'd be smart to book your flight now. Summer is almost ~~hear~~ *here* and you are not the only kid on the block who'll be heading south.

Do you ~~no~~ *know* what happens every time you take a step, cross your legs, or stoop to tie your shoe? Your knees are working hard. knees are among the most ~~vulnarable~~ *vulnerable* joints in the body. They take a great deal of stress every day, and they absorb much of the impact from ~~runing~~ *running* or jogging. To ~~increese~~ *increase* your knee strength, boost the surrounding ~~mussles~~ *muscles*, which act as a support system. You can Strengthen these muscles by doing exercises, such as knee extensions, wall squats, and hamstring curls. Maintaning a a healthy weight ~~an~~ *and* wearing the a proper footwear while walking jogging *or* will also help you maintain healthy knee ~~jonts~~ *joints*. the next time you ~~you~~ step onto that skateboard or run down a basketball court, remember how hard your knees are working for you. Take good care of them!